focus!

THE
POWER OF
PEOPLE
GROUP
THINKING

*A practical manual
for planning effective
strategies to reach
the unreached*

John D. Robb

Way to to eern

Genes.s 12:3

Galatians 3:8

Matt 18.19-20

MARC

FOCUS! The Power of People Group Thinking
John D. Robb

ISBN 0-912552-66-2

(626) $303-8811$

MARC books are published by World Vision, 800 West Chestnut Avenue, Monrovia, California 91016-3198, U.S.A.

Printed in the United States of America. Cover design: Edler Graphics.

Now printed in 14 languages: Bambara, Bengali, Chinese, English, French, Gujerati, Hindi, Japanese, Korean, Marathi, Oriya, Portuguese, Russian and Spanish; also available in overseas English editions for India and the Philippines. Contact John Robb at above address for specific information.

First printing: 1989
Second printing: 1994
Third printing: 1997
Fourth printing: 1999

to Lori

Without her selfless support, our service in behalf of the unreached peoples would not be possible.

Acknowledgments

I have received insightful contributions to the writing of this book from many friends and colleagues both at MARC (World Vision's Mission Advanced Research and Communication Center) and in the wider missions community. Ed Dayton, Dayton Roberts, Viggo Søgaard, and Harvie Conn were especially helpful in critiquing the original manuscript. Mitali Perkins, Betsy Dodge, Ken Graff and Richard Sears gave much valued assistance with formatting text, pictures, and diagrams. They all deserve my hearty thanks.

It has been a great privilege to facilitate Unreached Peoples seminars and conferences in 80 countries. Special appreciation must go to the many thousands of Christian workers with whom I have shared this material. As "iron sharpens iron," so I have learned as much or more from them as they have received from me.

Above all, I want to thank God for His continual grace and goodness as well as for the marvelous privilege of serving Him through World Vision's Unreached Peoples program.

John Robb
Monrovia, California
September 1994

Table of Contents

Introduction. 1

ONE: Focusing to reach unreached people groups

What is a "people group"? 7
What is "people group thinking"? 13
Some advantages to this approach 21
Research and people groups 29
Planning a strategy that works 37

TWO: Practical procedures for people group thinking

Surveying documents and experts 63
The participatory evaluation process 65
The ethnographic approach. 69
Sharing the results of your research 89

THREE: Releasing God's power through prayer

Prayer releases God's power
for mission to the unreached 95
Nine compelling reasons to pray. 103
The challenge of linking the global
prayer movement with frontier missions 129

FOUR: Networking the whole church

Networks link Christian
workers for outreach. 137
What is networking?. 141
Getting practical 147

A Final Word. 157
Endnotes 159
Questionnaire 165

Introduction

If you have a heart for mission, this book is written for you! It has been put together for the Christian who shares Christ's heartbeat for the peoples of the world—who senses their needs and feels their pain. It is designed for you if you want to see the love, justice and salvation of Jesus Christ begin to operate within a particular group of people for whom you are specially concerned.

If you are a missionary, an evangelist, a pastor or a lay person who wants to focus your ministry and to become more effective in God's service, this book can help you. It will give you the tools to develop a ministry strategy that will be relevant to the people you are trying to reach. It will enable you to communicate the gospel with new effectiveness and greater impact. And it will assist you to design programs of social service that the Spirit of God can use to move a whole unreached group toward the salvation and social well-being He so deeply desires for them.

A bit of history

During the last quarter of this century, the evangelical missions movement has become increasingly captivated by the prospect of taking the good news of Christ to all of the world's remaining unreached peoples. Some mission leaders have hoped to accomplish this as early as the year 2000.

The contemporary concern for unreached peoples burst into prominence at the Lausanne Congress on World Evangelization in 1974 through the country-by-country research efforts of MARC and a provocative plenary address by Ralph Winter. Since then the unreached peoples concept has increasingly been used by the Holy Spirit to call the attention of the Church to its unfinished task—the evangelization of up to two billion people cut off from hearing the gospel by barriers of culture and language, or because of political considerations.

Mission agencies have been challenged to rethink their strategies and redeploy their workers. Young people by the thousands are again hearing the call to cross-cultural missionary service. For all of this, we should praise God and exult in this new major awakening of missionary endeavor, due in large part to a fresh focus on the unreached peoples.

Unreachedness—to be aware is not enough

Emphasis on the unreachedness of these peoples, their isolation from hearing of the grace and love of Christ, is what has provided much of the motivating force for mobilizing this new mission effort. Prayer, missionary recruitment, fund-raising, research, have all been accelerated by the grim reality of whole groups of people in danger of perdition and without opportunity to receive a clear gospel witness.

But emphasizing the unreachedness of peoples, while it stirs up very real and essential concern for the lost, does not give us any practical guidance on how to reach them. And this is ultimately the direction in which true missionary concern must take us. How do we reach the unreached peoples?

Because we have often stressed the "unreached" half of the term "unreached peoples," many of us have failed to see the significance of the peoplehood of these peoples—the fact that the unreached exist as distinct groups of people. And it is in their "people groupness"—in those unique characteristics that make people a group—that we will find the key to understanding how to actually reach them.

In thinking of the unreached as people groups, we will discover a powerful model for planning effective ministries that God will use to impact whole groups with the gospel of Christ.

What you can expect to find here

The purpose of this booklet is to provide a basic orientation for what we will call "people group thinking."

If we are to minister effectively to the unreached, it stands to reason we must learn all we can about those people we aim to serve. Only in this way can we design ministries appropriate to their unique cultures and their particular situations along the path of the journey towards Christ and His Kingdom. Planning ministries that meet the deepest needs, both physical and spiritual, of our target groups is what this booklet is all about.

When you have mastered the contents of the following pages and worked through the exercises provided, you should know the answers to these questions:

- What is a "people group"?
- What is "people group thinking"?
- What are the values of the people group approach for planning various ministries?
- How do we research a people group in the field and come to understand people from the inside out?
- In what ways can we best communicate the Good News of Jesus Christ to them?
- How do we plan ministries that God can use to move whole groups of people towards a better future—one that includes a Kingdom life-style of enhanced socioeconomic dignity?
- What part does prayer play in the reaching of unreached people groups?
- Why and how does prayer release God's powerful working among them?
- Why should we network with other segments of Christ's Church?
- How can a cooperative ministry network be developed for a people group I am concerned about?

Author's note: Through the privilege of interacting with Christian workers in many parts of the world over the last several years, I have become increasingly convinced that mission strategies, no matter how creative and relevant to the people group concerned, will almost certainly fail unless coupled with ongoing prayerful dependence on God and cooperative interdependence with others who share our ministry vision. In the 1990s there is a growing recognition among those Christians committed to both the Great Commission and the Great Commandment that we must pray together and work together as never before if the lost and the poor are to hear His voice and feel His touch.

We are currently witnessing the development of an enormous global prayer movement focussed on the unevangelized world, especially those sixty or so countries which make up "the 10/40 Window," that belt of nations between 10 and 40 degrees north latitude, running from northwest Africa through the Middle East to Central and South Asia, where the great majority of unreached peoples are found. For the first time in the history of Christianity many millions of Christians are being joined together through advanced telecommunications, sharing the same information to guide their intercession. At the same time there is deepening acceptance throughout the body of Christ that denominational and organizational labels are becoming less and less important as we are caught up together in the larger cause of making Christ known to those who have never encountered Him.

In light of all God is doing to bring His people together, it is my earnest conviction that united prayer and deliberate networking, though not glamorous, high-profile activities, are the twin keys to effective mission and ultimately the evangelization of the whole world. It was out of this conviction that parts three and four have been added to the original text of *Focus! The Power of People Group Thinking.*

Part One

FOCUSING TO REACH UNREACHED PEOPLE GROUPS

What is a "People Group?"

We are a map-oriented society. It is not surprising, therefore, that normally we look at the world from a geopolitical standpoint as made of up of many nations. Less often we think of the world as composed of many peoples - large ethnolinguistic groupings of those who share a similar overall culture and a common language. But usually we do not see that each nation and people is composed of a great diversity of *people groups*. Both nations and peoples are generally too large and undifferentiated to be useful categories for developing adequately focused ministry strategies. However, if we concentrate on one segment of a people -- a people group -- effective strategizing becomes practicable.

For example, to target the whole Crown Colony of Hong Kong or even Cantonese Chinese with one strategy is not workable since there are so many different sub-groups, or what we have chosen to call people groups, that make up these larger population segments. Each group has its own occupation(s), social classes, dialect differences, and unique way of life.

To design a strategy for the 150,000 Cantonese-speaking restaurant workers of Hong Kong makes more sense since they constitute a definite people group with their own specialized forms of communication and job behavior. Other people groups in Hong Kong, such as new

Diagram #1
PEOPLE GROUP CONCEPT

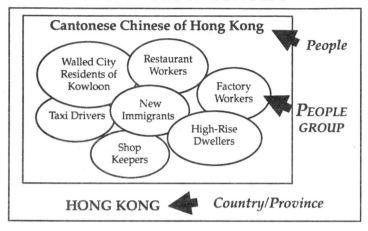

immigrants from China, factory workers, taxi drivers, drug addicts, and residents of the walled city will also need their own relevant approaches.

What then exactly is a people group? A people group is a "significantly large grouping of individuals who perceive themselves to have a common affinity for one another, because of their shared language, religion, ethnicity, residence, occupation, class or caste, situation, or combinations of these." From the standpoint of communicating the message of Christ, it is "the largest group within which the gospel can flow along natural lines without encountering barriers of understanding or acceptance due to culture, language, geography, etc."[2]

Notice that this definition emphasizes the things a group of people hold *in common* and that act as boundaries which set this group apart from other groups. Of course, individual members within any social group often differ from one another in many ways -- how they look, how they dress, in preference for certain foods, sports and hobbies. The point of our definition is that there are certain overarching similarities such as those named above that cause all individuals to feel at home in one group as opposed to another.

These cultural, linguistic and other similarities are the basis upon which people communicate, interact and influence one another's values and way of life. They give a group of people their special sense of identity, that sense of being "we" as opposed to "they." They also are the dimensions that need to be identified and incorporated into any evangelistic strategy.

- The Dema, a group of hunter-gatherers living in a remote area of the African country of Zimbabwe, have a strong sense of groupness. When one child was mistreated in a government school, the whole group pulled up their encampments and emigrated elsewhere.
- The Dabawallahs of Bombay jealously guard their niche in society as the premier hot lunch delivery men of the city. Only fellow workers from their own occupation caste are welcome to join them. Outsiders applying for employment do not stand a chance of being accepted in this close-knit group.
- The garbage collectors of Seoul, Korea live and work together in their own communal area. They are suspicious of and impervious to outsiders who want to make contact.

These are just a few examples of the myriad of people groups found throughout the world and in every society and nation. India alone has 3,000 major ethnic groups and castes that can be further broken down into many thousands of more distinct people groups such as the Dabawallahs above.

The City of Los Angeles in the United States has become home to well over 100 language groups from around the globe. In one sense these are ethnolinguistic peoples, but actually within broader language groupings are many more distinct people groups.

EXERCISES

Spend a few minutes thinking about the place where you live and work. Using the above definition of a people group, how many distinct people groups can you identify? Make a list of as many as possible for your society.

Much of our work of serving Christ is aimed at communities as geographically-bounded societies. Is a people group the same thing as a community? Yes and no. If we understand a community in its root meaning as people with common characteristics and interests who may live together in a particular area, we are probably talking about a people group. However, a community is often understood (or misunderstood) more in a geographical sense as a village or town than in its primary idea of social interaction based on common identity.

This is where confusion may arise for us as missionaries and development workers. A village or town may be inhabited by more than one people group. When we move into an urban or rural area to minister to its residents, it is therefore essential to the impact, appropriateness, and success of our ministry that we become conscious of the diversity of people groups that may be present, rather than unwittingly lump them all together according to geographical criteria alone.

What is "People Group Thinking?"

People group thinking is an approach to ministry. It refers to that process by which those engaged in evangelism and/or social service first become conscious of the diversity of people groups in their society. They then design and carry out ministry efforts that take into account the uniqueness of the particular group or groups with which they have chosen to work.

Though the phrase is of our own modern concoction, the concept, we believe, has its roots in God's strategy for bringing redemption to the human race. Originally it emanates from Yahweh's redemptive purpose which clearly encompasses all the people groups of His world. From the call of Abraham in Genesis 12 onward through Bible history, God's concern has always been that the blessing of His redemption flow to all peoples and to the people groups within them.

The Hebrew word *mishpaha* in Genesis 12:3, often translated either as "families" (KJV) or "peoples" (NIV), can be more accurately rendered by an in-between social category like "communities" or "people groups." One noted Hebrew scholar, E. A. Speiser, author of the Anchor Bible Commentary on Genesis, rejects the most commonly translated "families" in favor of "communities." According to him, *mishpaha's* basic meaning is "category, class or subdivision with the accent being on the idea of 'political communities.'" The word "families," he thinks, would have been expressed by another Hebrew term.[3]

Richard Showalter affirms that this term is "most commonly used to describe a subdivision of a tribe or larger people group...it is a social group smaller than a tribe, but larger than a household."[4] William Holladay's Hebrew lexicon agrees that *mishpaha* in Genesis 12:3 is best translated as "subdivisions of ethnic and national groups."[5]

In the rest of Scripture, *mishpaha* is capable of considerable flexibility and latitude of usage, depending upon its context. It is translated ethnically as "clan," "tribe" or "people." It is used sociologically as "kind" or "classes." In at least one instance it is used occupationally as "guild."[6]

Notice how this usage parallels what has been said about the people group model for viewing humankind. People groups are bound together by those things they hold in common. They are communities in the true sense of that word, partaking in a common life together.

People groups are also colored by shared ethnic or tribal characteristics, though they are generally *subdivisions* of such larger categories. They may, in addition, be united by such things as shared occupation, place of residence and/or social class.

In saying these things, we are not necessarily arguing for a tight one-to-one correlation between the terms *mishpaha* and people group. Nor are we saying that the early Hebrews were sociological theorists in advance of their time. We are instead contending that people group thinking is not just a modern sociological construct, but has its roots in the way that our Creator-Redeemer looks at His world and envisions His redemptive blessing reaching all of it.

Working from the inside out

Those who learn to think in people group terms realize the importance of coming to understand their target group *before* planning any ministry to reach them. They start with the people to be ministered to rather than a program to be administered. They see the value of research before action. They come as learners willing to be taught by the members of the community, to enter into their experience and see life through *their* eyes.

Such Christian workers have an incarnational attitude -- a willingness to divest themselves of their preconceptions and the baggage of their own cultural background in order to identify themselves humbly with the culture of the target group. They design their strategy from *within* the context, rather than bring their set solutions to it.

Jesus spent almost 30 years humbly identifying with His people group, the Aramaic-speaking Galilean Jews of Nazareth. Living and working among them as a member of the community, He entered fully into their experience and unique way of looking at life. His teaching ministry that followed bears ample witness to His acute, empathetic understanding of this people group. His parables, drawn as they were from the rustic lifestyle of the Galilean towns and countryside, enthralled His hearers as no sermons have since.

The Apostle Paul deliberately accommodated his way of living and presentation of the gospel to the particular group he was seeking to win for Christ (1 Corinthians 9:20): "To those under the law, I became like one under the law (though I myself am not under the law) so as to win those under the law." In other words, he started with a people group he was trying to reach, attempting to communicate the gospel in a way that took into account their particular world view and thought forms. Compare his ministry approaches to the Athenian intellectuals (Acts 17:22-31), idolatrous Lystrans (Acts 14:15-17) and orthodox Jews (Acts 13:16-41). It could be said that in his determination to understand and accommodate to his target group, Paul was instinctively practicing "people group thinking."

Matteo Ricci showed us how

Matteo Ricci, the sixteenth century Jesuit pioneer missionary to China, spent 20 years identifying with and coming to understand the people group he had chosen to reach. The Mandarins were the elite class of scholar-administrators that had ruled the nation for centuries. Recognizing that they would be an extremely strategic group upon which to concentrate ministry, due to their far-reaching influence, Ricci was willing to pay the price of mastering the Confucian classics along with Chinese history and philosophy in order to comprehend his target group's world view and to communicate Christ within their frame of reference.

In this painstaking manner, he and his Jesuit colleagues managed to develop close relationships with many of the scholars. They succeeded in winning large numbers of literate, influential friends for the gospel throughout China and made converts even among the top rulers of the country. Ultimately, through Ricci's successors, even the emperor of China was brought face-to-face with the claims of Christ and almost personally embraced the Christian faith.

Ricci's ministry is a vivid, compelling illustration of the power of people group thinking, of the importance of clearly defining a particular group we feel we ought to reach and attempting to learn as much as possible about them so as to minister effectively to them.

Tragically, two other orders, the Franciscans and Dominicans, later entered China without the careful, well thought-out people group focus of Ricci and his associates. They did not bother to learn the language or ways of the Chinese, but instead immediately began preaching in the streets, holding crucifixes aloft and calling upon their perplexed Chinese hearers to repent.

The Franciscans and Dominicans' blatant insensitivity and stubborn unwillingness to understand and accommodate themselves to Chinese cultural practices were certainly major factors in later disputes with the Jesuits and eventual development of the Rites Controversy, a disagreement between the missionaries and the Vatican about the participation of converts in rites of ancestral veneration. Sadly, it was this latter historical development that caused the then emperor to expel all missionaries from China, repudiate Christianity and bring ruin to the Chinese church.

It is still happening

I was among a number of graduate students and community volunteers who learned the power of people group thinking in planning ministry to young people in a suburb of Chicago during the mid-1970's. We had noticed the many youth who aimlessly wandered the city on weekend nights, often getting embroiled in acts of vandalism, dope dealing and other crimes. We decided to renovate an old house near the city center to serve as a drop-in place where young people could gather out of harm's way to enjoy each other's company, listen to Christian musical performers, and eat free popcorn.

Our staff of adult volunteers sought to accept the young people as they were, endeavoring to love, understand and listen to them so that we could fashion a relevant Christian response. Almost unconsciously, in our efforts to empathize and accommodate ourselves to the youth subculture, we were practicing people group thinking. The results were apparent. Many nights 70-80 youth with tousled hair, often smelling of marijuana and alcohol, descended on that old house like bees to honey.

Other examples of people group oriented ministries could be multiplied from around the world: Prison Fellowship's work with prisoners, Teen Challenge's programs for drug addicts, Grass Roots Mission's efforts among Taipei's taxi drivers, or YWAM's mission to the prostitutes of Amsterdam. No doubt you could mention many more.

The important thing to note in all such ministries is that "people group thinkers" allow for ministry plans, projects and programs to spring forth from this incarnational process of entering into a community and coming to *understand* them. Having comprehended where they have been and where they are in their journey towards God's better future, Christian workers can design ministries that He can use to take them further along in this direction.

Instead of acting inappropriately and insensitively, they can respond relevantly and pointedly to the peculiar felt needs of their target group. No more are they shooting in the dark and hoping somehow to hit the target.

QUESTIONS

Do I really understand the community among which I am ministering or planning to minister? Have I put programs before people, action before learning? What changes of attitude and action will be necessary for me to make in order to more humbly identify with the people group I want to reach?

_____

_____

_____

_____

_____

_____

_____

_____

_____

_____

_____

_____

_____

_____

_____

_____

_____

_____

_____

_____

_____

_____

_____

Some advantages to this approach

For those who want to minister more effectively to people, there are a number of clear advantages of what we call people group thinking.

Ministry can become holistic

People group thinking better ensures that ministry to our target group will be **holistic**. Much has been said about the need to bring evangelism and social responsibility into better balance, and yet Christians are still divided over the relationship between the two, and particularly how the two can be kept integrated in one ministry.[7] More recently we have been faced with the role of signs and wonders and power encounters and how they fit together with word and deed. Unfortunately, these three elements of Christian ministry are sometimes thought to be mutually exclusive.

Evangelists tend to stress proclamation of the gospel message, development workers emphasize works of mercy, and Charismatic healers the supernatural and miraculous dimensions of ministry.

The people group approach enables holistic ministry to take place without forcing evangelism, power encounter and social service into an either/or dichotomy or trichotomy. As we come to understand our target community in the totality of their life-way and felt needs, we will be better able to respond in a way that enables all three to be naturally integrated.

The proportions of the mix will depend on where the people group is in its journey towards the Kingdom. In some situations, such as with a resistant Muslim group, it may be necessary to de-emphasize overt evangelism in favor of a greater stress on works of mercy until practical Christian caring has moved the group along to a greater openness to the gospel. A quiet, unobtrusive witness shining through loving deeds of service is obviously the way to go in such a situation. Or, in the case of an animistic tribe living in the fear of evil spirits, power encounter through healing or exorcism may need to precede and authenticate the preached word.

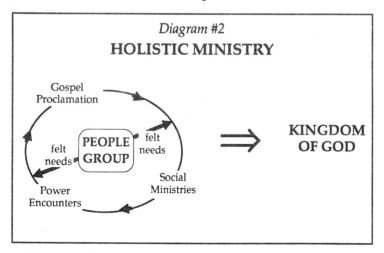

The people group approach enables us to go beyond the fear or guilt which many feel at having to stress evangelism, charismatic gifts, or social caring over and against each other. All are valuable in differing proportions, depending on our target group's position in the process of becoming all that God wants them to be.

A missionary to the Masai tribe of Kenya perceived the felt needs of this group to be education and health care. By building schools and providing clinics, he met their felt socioeconomic needs, and as a by-product, their previously resistant attitude towards the Christian faith has been changing. In recent years he has been able to stress evangelism in an all-out manner, and the Masai are now undergoing a significant people movement to Christ.

QUESTIONS

Are there churches, missions or development agencies in your country that have effectively integrated evangelism, signs and wonders ministry and social service? If so, how have they been able to achieve this? If they haven't, how might a clear people group focus enable them to better keep evangelism, social caring and signs/wonders ministry in better balance?

_____

_____

_____

_____

_____

_____

_____

_____

_____

_____

_____

_____

_____

_____

_____

_____

_____

_____

_____

_____

_____

_____

_____

_____

_____

It is more manageable

The people group approach makes ministry **manageable**. It breaks down the enormous task of reaching the world for Christ into manageable segments. David Barrett has estimated that humankind may be composed of around 9,000 separate ethnolinguistic peoples.[8] If this is so, there may be as many as 25,000 to 40,000 distinct people groups. We do not know exactly. But whether there are 25,000 or 40,000, there are a finite number of human groups to be served with the gospel.

As in major industries, where the most complex production processes are broken down into hundreds or thousands of segments, so utilizing the people group approach, we can simplify the colossal job of ministering to a needy world of over three billion unreached individuals. For a worldwide church of 1.7 billion professing Christians to send out 25,000 or even 40,000 cross-cultural mission teams is not impossible, given the immense resources of gifted people and finance with which God has blessed His Church. World evangelization suddenly becomes easier to visualize and manage!

With this approach, different agencies and churches can see where they fit into the worldwide ministry of the Body of Christ. They can determine what groups are the neediest and prioritize them accordingly. It is easier to see which groups they could best help, given their own organizational strengths. They can better coordinate their efforts with other agencies to avoid duplication of precious resources and services.

You can measure it

People group thinking makes the ministry of the worldwide church **measurable**. With research, we can identify those groups the Body of Christ has already been effective in helping. We can measure the advancement of God's Kingdom as people groups turn from spiritual darkness to light and experience His *shalom* of social and physical well-being. Tracking progress in this way will enable churches and agencies to stay on course, redirecting their ministry to others when those people groups to which they have previously directed themselves no longer need the same attention.

It is the strategic way

People group thinking is **strategic**. Instead of trying to reach every individual in our target group ourselves, outsiders can establish a cross-cultural beachhead by ministering in-depth to some. We then trust the Holy Spirit to use the resulting believers, who as cultural insiders can help their own people more effectively than we ever could. This is particularly important for those people groups still unreached by the spread of the gospel, since perhaps 80 percent of non-Christians are separated by language and cultural barriers from churches and agencies that could reach them.

Such thinking is also strategic because it focuses the attention of the Church on the unfinished task. As people groups in need are uncovered and their needs clarified, Christians are moved to respond by lifting up their eyes to see fields white for harvest and to pray the Lord of the harvest to send laborers into that harvest. In this manner, people group thinking is used by God to multiply ministry because through it He burdens believers to get involved in meeting the needs of the world.

It encourages people movements

People group thinking also encourages **people movements** to Christ. Donald McGavran's church growth research revealed that the great majority of conversions to the Christian faith have come through "people movements." According to him:

> (A people group movement results from) the joint decision of a number of individuals -- whether five or 500 -- all from the same people which enables them to become Christians without social dislocation while remaining in full contact with their non-Christian relatives, thus enabling other groups of that people across the years after suitable instruction to come to similar decisions and form Christian churches made up exclusively of members of that people.[9]

As McGavran has convincingly demonstrated here and elsewhere in his writings, people movements minimize the tremendous social and cultural barriers to the conversion of unreached groups.

People group thinking encourages the emergence of people movements and the effective harvesting of whole groups of people for the Kingdom because it respects the social relationships and decision-making processes within a society. It enables Christian workers to keep their focus upon winning the whole group rather than just isolated members of it. This kind of thinking opens the door to the possibility of much more vigorous church growth since whole segments of a society are brought to Christ with their culture and social structures more or less intact.

Kenneth Scott Latourette was obviously thinking in these terms when he wrote:

> More and more we must dream in terms of winning groups, not merely individuals. Too often with our Protestant, nineteenth-century individualism, we have torn men and women one by one out of the family, village, or clan with the result that they have been permanently de-racinated and maladjusted....Experience shows that it is much better if an entire natural group -- a family, village, caste or tribe -- can come rapidly over into the faith. That gives reinforcement to the individual Christian and makes easier the Christianization of the entire life of the community.[10]

People group thinking makes possible the winning of whole groups because it constantly sees the immediate conversion of individuals in relationship to the ultimate reaching of their entire social group. That is why it could be said that people group thinkers have a "harvest mentality" -- a concern for reaping a whole society for Christ segment by segment, much as a farmer would bring in his crop field by field. And it is certain that only this kind of "whole group" mentality and the holistic evangelistic approaches that flow from it will be successful in winning significant portions of the great unreached blocs of humankind.

QUESTIONS

Think of some other advantages or values of the people group approach to ministry. How might this approach be beneficial to the work of ministry in your society? To your own ministry?

_____
_____
_____
_____
_____
_____
_____
_____
_____
_____
_____
_____
_____
_____
_____
_____
_____
_____
_____
_____
_____
_____
_____

Research and People Groups

The imperative of understanding

Coming to understand the people group we want to reach is critical for planning and for ministry itself. If we are to meet their deepest needs in the power of Christ, we need to do our homework. It is surprising how many missionary endeavors and development efforts begin without sufficient understanding of their target groups. History is littered with well-intentioned projects that went awry because they were inappropriate or caused outright offense to the receiving group, thus nullifying their noble purposes. What is the answer? How can we acquire such understanding? People group thinking helps us understand where to begin and what kind of research is needed.

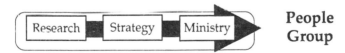

People Group

The value of research for ministry

The word "research" has an intimidatingly academic ring to it that can scare off even the most studious of Christian workers. In our mind's eye we see images of laboratories filled with an assortment of glass beakers and exotic gadgets for experimentation. Or, we imagine furrow-browed scholars squinting over musty manuscripts, submerged in piles of books and documents. But research for ministry need not conform to this forbidding stereotype. Research for the development of more effective ministry can be a practical, down-to-earth activity in which all of us are capable of engaging. It basically consists of getting the necessary facts about the people group we intend to minister to in order to develop ministries that will be relevant to where they are, that will scratch where they are itching, so to speak.

Many busy missionary and development workers who are already over-burdened with the incessant demands of ongoing ministry may doubt the value of investing time and effort in a research endeavor. Perhaps you have your own reservations on this score. Are we not supposed to be out preaching the gospel and caring for the needy?

Research, some may feel, if it is a valid part of Christian work, is somehow a less spiritual, even worldly, approach to doing ministry. Certainly it is less valuable, we might reason, than engaging in the actual activity of meeting the needs of people.

But there is biblical precedent for putting research before action and, according to Scripture, this priority sprang from the command of God.

In Numbers 13:1-3, God commanded Moses to send out a band of researchers to survey the land of Canaan and its peoples:

> The Lord said to Moses, send some men to explore the land of Canaan which I am giving to the Israelites. From each ancestral tribe send one of the leaders. So *at the Lord's command*, Moses sent them out... (emphasis mine)

God commanded that the Israelites research the land and its peoples *before* attempting to enter because they needed to have factual information in order to develop effective military strategies and successfully conquer these peoples. It is true that their mission, the elimination of Canaan's wicked inhabitants, is quite different from ours, the evangelization of unreached people groups. But the principle of putting research before action remains the same.

Notice that Moses sent the twelve spies out with a list of specific questions to be answered. Numbers 13:17-20 reads as follows:

> When Moses sent them to explore Canaan he said, "Go up through the Negev and into the hill country. See what the land is like and whether the people who live there are strong or weak, few or many. What kind of land do they live in? Is it good or bad? What kind of towns do they live in? Are they unwalled or fortified? How is the soil? Is it fertile or poor? Are there trees on it or not?"

There may have been other questions Moses gave them to answer. This is probably just a brief summary. But there are two important points to note. First, this research survey was a God-conceived project that would be of crucial relevance to their mission -- taking possession of the land of Canaan. Second, the research endeavor was given a priority in time to the activity of the later conquest.

Why does so much of today's ministry go astray, ineffectively falling on deaf ears? One reason could be that we have ignored this research priority and plunged into service without first understanding our target people.

Research is not something unspiritual or irrelevant to the business of ministry. It is rather the essential foundation for strategic, effective ministry. If we do not first come to understand the people we seek to reach, how can we plan to communicate the gospel in a way that strikes a responsive cord, that makes sense to them in their unique life situation and particular vexing needs? It is like shooting in the dark and hoping that if we fire in enough different directions, one shot may hit the bullseye. Someone has amusingly described much contemporary Christian communication:

> Christian communication is like a blunderbuss.
> For all our muss and fuss,
> We fire a monstrous charge of shot,
> And sometimes hit, but mostly not.[11]

QUESTIONS

Reflect on your own feelings about research. What reservations do you have about engaging in it? What other values do you see in research-based ministry? What research (if any) is being done on the people groups in your nation? How are churches and agencies making or not making use of it?

_____

_____

_____

_____

_____

_____

_____

_____

_____

_____

_____

Developing strategy from research

Having asserted the value of giving research priority in ministry, it is also necessary to emphasize that ministry-related research never be allowed to become an end in itself. It is a common failing of many research efforts to accumulate information for information's sake, losing sight of the original purpose of the data-gathering. Some estimates are that up to 50 percent of research in the business world ends up collecting dust on a shelf and exerts no impact on corporate decision-making. It is essential to realize that the research data gathered in Numbers was *used* to develop military strategy in Joshua. Joshua, the researcher, later became Joshua, the general. Even military scientists of today recognize the brilliant strategist he was.

As Christian workers, our stress should be on *applied* research -- in only doing the amount of research necessary to develop a sound ministry strategy. We have found that a better question to guide research efforts is, "What difference does it make?" rather than, "How well can I know it?" In other words, we should be interested not just in amassing a body of knowledge, but in seeing the data's implications for ministry.

Research needs to give rise to strategy, which in turn results in actual, enhanced ministry. One good definition of applied research is that it is an effort to supply missing experience, experience we will need to do the task.

A national unreached peoples project for a nation in Africa was completed a couple of years ago. The researchers did a superb job of identifying unreached people groups, gathering data on these groups and publishing marvelous volumes based on their work. Unfortunately, the research was not done by those who would use it -- the church workers and evangelists -- so, until recently, most of it remained on library shelves, unused for the work on the field.

Because the researchers were not involved in the work of field ministry, they never made the transition from research to strategy to ministry. By contrast, a survey done of an African city secured the cooperation and sponsorship of the churches in the city well in advance, and then fed them results as things progressed. The churches became vitally interested in the research process and incorporated its findings into their ongoing ministries.

Research findings need to be in the hands of those Christian workers who will actually use them in ministry. It is imperative that even before the research commences, those who will use the findings decide how the results will be used to guide ministry efforts. How is what we will learn about this people group going to affect the way we minister to them? What do we need to know to develop a sound strategy for reaching them? What is it we don't know that we need to know? How much can we learn *before* we begin ministry?

In order to keep from being sidetracked by the myriad of possible research pursuits involving the people group we have chosen to study, it is necessary from the very outset that we determine our precise research purpose and the kinds of data we will need to fulfill that purpose. One seasoned researcher bemoans the ambiguity of objectives that characterizes so much research endeavor:

> It is an 'occupational trait' of research novices to want to 'study the world,' the so-called shotgun approach to research....Failure to define efficiently leads to amassing cupboards full of data.[12]

If our purpose is to develop an effective ministry to a local people group, we will need to confine ourselves to gathering information that bears directly on that objective. Understanding the decision-making process of the group may be germane to our quest, but knowing how they like their favorite foods prepared may not be. It is helpful to turn our purpose into a question; indeed, the whole research process involves asking the right questions to acquire the special kinds of information required. Using the example above, we might formulate our question in this way: "What are the particular characteristics of the group that will affect the way we approach them with the gospel?"

You will think of your own way of phrasing your research question, but the important thing is to *do it* because it will keep you focused on your exact purpose. Don Douglas, a former colleague at MARC, adds this insight:

> The questions that one asks in pursuing answers are of utmost importance. Often, we are not really clear about what it is we want or need to know. This is because we have not refined adequately the central question regarding what we are trying to discover.

A lack of clarity or fuzziness in the statement of the question that we are addressing will produce fuzzy results.

Perhaps more Christian research has been less than useful for this reason than any other. What is needed by way of information is ill-conceived because we do not know exactly what it is we need to know. Consequently, there is little usable result in our attempt at research. The point is to sharpen the question and limit it, so that it addresses our need precisely. A shotgun approach does not result in rifle accuracy when it comes to research.[13]

EXERCISES

Take a few minutes now to reflect on the people group you have chosen. What do you need to know to plan a strategy to reach them? Write your research purpose and then turn it into a specific research question.

_____

_____

_____

_____

_____

_____

_____

_____

_____

_____

_____

_____

_____

_____

Turn to Part Two for a treatment of practical procedures for researching a people group in the field.

Planning a strategy that works

Once we have come to understand a people group through research we are in a better position to develop a strategy to minister to them. But what is a strategy? Why is it important to have one? And how do we go about designing one?

Just what is a strategy?

What is a strategy? The dictionary defines it as a careful plan, or more specifically, the art of devising or employing plans to reach a goal.

Originally the word comes from a Greek term meaning "generalship," that is the science and art of military command exercised to meet an enemy in combat. We could sum up the military idea of the word as the careful planning necessary to fight a war in order to attain the ultimate goal of victory.

Most of us have seen war movies in which the general or admiral pictured was studying a chart on the wall and considering how the whole operation ought to be conducted. Failure to plan maneuvers carefully, foresee dangers, and above all, keep the final objective in view will result in disaster and ultimate defeat. Even though successful in winning some smaller skirmishes, the commander will lose the war. Good strategy, therefore, is related to long-range planning and foresight.

We practice strategic planning not only in war but in all areas of life. Even in marriage, we (or our parents) employ a strategy in finding the right partner for us. In such a consequential matter no one can afford not to exercise foresight and plan properly. At one stage in my pre-marital days, I became infatuated with a young woman without thinking clearly ahead what marriage with her would be like, particularly since I had felt God's call into missions. My wise old pastor took me aside one day and said, "John, there are worse things than being single!" With his cooler, calmer perspective he could see my pursuit of her would be a bad marriage strategy.

We utilize strategy, whether consciously or not, in deciding the career we will pursue, how many children we will have and how they will be educated. We want to make wise decisions because of the long-range effects they will have upon us and our families, so we think and plan carefully beforehand the best way of accomplishing life goals. This is strategy.

How it can enhance your ministry

Having said all this, it is strange that many Christian workers do not have a clear strategy for ministry. Many of us do not employ long-range planning, foreseeing where we want to be, what we want to have accomplished one year, five years or ten years down the road. We are busy preaching the gospel, carrying out social service activities of one sort or another -- and this is good -- but we do not know where, besides heaven, we ultimately want to arrive.

Several years ago, while serving in Malaysia, I gave my time and involvement, along with other Christian leaders, to a mass media evangelistic campaign. It was reported to have been highly successful in other cities so we decided to lend it our support. Many pastors and churches were involved and gave heavily of their time, energy and money.

The campaign appealed to a certain segment of the population -- English-educated young people -- and there were many "decisions" from among this group. However, very few became disciples and were integrated into the churches. On top of that, 50 percent of the population, the Muslims, were incensed by this culturally insensitive approach.

If we pastors and missionaries had thought strategically and exercised foresight in visualizing the probable impact of the campaign, as far as the likely number of disciples that would be made and the adverse reaction by the Malay Muslims, we would not have employed this standard, pre-packaged approach to our unique, culturally diverse city. We would have developed long-range evangelistic strategies for each of the distinct social and cultural groups that took into account their uniqueness as groups.

Diagram #4

A MODEL FOR MINISTRY TO A PEOPLE GROUP

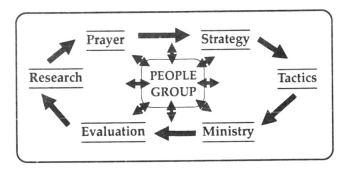

When we busy ourselves with ministry activities without taking the time to do long-range planning, we are applying tactics without strategy. "Tactics" is another military term. It is defined as a method of employing forces in combat, such as when infantry movements are deployed to secure a particular section of the battlefield. Good tactics are important. No war can be won without them. However, they need the overall direction that a strategy supplies. Otherwise, they form a chain of unrelated, uncoordinated events that do not contribute to that one supreme purpose we are trying to achieve.

Strategy informs and guides tactics so that each tactical action counts. The Apostle Paul was talking about the relationship of strategy and tactics when he affirmed that he didn't "run like a man running aimlessly" or "fight like a man beating the air" (1 Corinthians 9:26). Each tactical activity, whether it was preaching, teaching or healing, he applied as part of a larger strategy to bring the peoples, the Gentiles of the Roman Empire, to faith in Jesus Christ. Tactics were important, but they had to fit into his long-range plan.

Today, most of us engaged in ministry are good tacticians, but we are generally weak as strategists. We may be gifted in sharing the gospel with individuals or from a platform. We may be effective in organizing relief, development or childcare programs, but have we ever sat down and, in thoughtful dependence on the Holy Spirit, drawn up a long-term strategy for our ministry? Many Christian workers have no such concept of strategy other than a vague notion of serving Christ and being His instrument to reach others for Him. It is not until we begin thinking and praying about what we would like to see accomplished in the future that a clear strategy of ministry will begin to crystallize.

Strategy is concerned about the future and what it ought to look like according to God's revealed purposes for mankind. One ministry strategist put it this way: "Strategy is an attempt to anticipate the future. (It is) our statement of faith as to what we believe the future should be like, and how we should go about reaching that future."[14]

Strategizing about the future is an act of faith. Many Christians feel it is presumptuous and unspiritual to carefully plan for the future. That is God's business. But it is clear from Scripture that both God and man have a part in bringing about the future. Proverbs 16:9 says, "The mind of a man plans his way, but the Lord directs his steps." God expects us to use our minds to plan our way in accordance with His revealed word. That's strategy.

As we implement our strategy, He promises to direct the outworking of that strategy, and perhaps modify it as we go, just as He did with Paul in his Macedonian vision experience. But the important thing is that a strategy provides us with direction as we travel towards the future. It is like a road map or a compass. Those who fly to other parts of the world travel on planes with precision maps and compasses enabling them to fly half way around the world across vast expanses of ocean and to land right on target at the airport. A ministry strategy will do the same for your service for Christ.

Strategizing about the future enables the building of new vision. From time to time, we need to use our imaginations to envision the limitless possibilities of God's working through us. Ephesians 3:20 says, "God is able to do far more abundantly than all we can ask or think, according to the power at work within us."

To paraphrase a statement of Cho Yonggi, pastor of the world's largest church in Korea: "God's people need to allow themselves to dream, that is to imagine what is the greatest thing God could do through me, then ask Him to do it and He will." Strategizing in faith about the future opens the door to new possibilities we have never dreamed of before.

Another form of direction a strategy provides is help in deciding what we will *not* do. There are a host of good activities that can soak up our time and divert us from that one most strategic objective. A strategy enables us to concentrate all our resources on what we have determined is the essential task we need to perform.

The apostle Paul was singleminded, even ruthless, in focusing all his efforts on completing the task God had given him (Acts 20:24). What is that one thing you ought to concentrate your whole being on attaining?

Clausewitz, the great Prussian military strategist, said something that is as true in evangelistic ministry as in war:

> The best strategy is always to be very strong...*at the decisive point*....There is no more imperative and no simpler law for strategy than to *keep the forces concentrated*. No portion is to be separated from the main body unless called away by some urgent necessity... all forces which are available and destined for a strategic object should be *simultaneously applied* to it... compressed into one act and one movement (emphasis mine).[15]

In the sense that ministry to needy people is a war of a different kind, we would do well to heed this admonition. We need to concentrate all our energies and efforts on what we have determined is the strategic, decisive object.

Diagram #5

STRATEGY MOVES US TOWARD THE GOAL

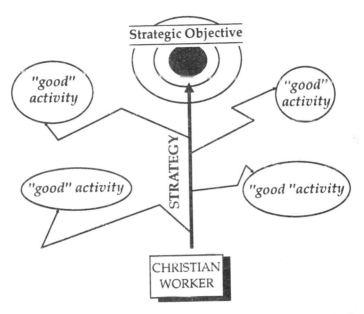

So how do we develop such a ministry strategy? Is there a planning model that will work with any people group?

Using the Søgaard Scale

Viggo Søgaard, building on the work of others, has developed the latest and most workable tool for plotting the position of a community in its spiritual journey and planning a ministry strategy to move them toward the Kingdom.[16] The Søgaard Scale also works just as well to picture a people group's progress towards a better socioeconomic future. For this reason, we can use it to plan a ministry that will be truly holistic, combining evangelism and social service into an integrated strategy.

The scale consists of two axes as pictured in Figure A. The vertical axis depicts the people group's knowledge of Christ and His gospel. The amount of knowledge increases as the axis moves upward. The horizontal axis describes their attitude towards what they know of Christ and His way. Degrees of negative attitude are pictured on the left; positive on the right.

Figure A
THE SØGAARD SCALE

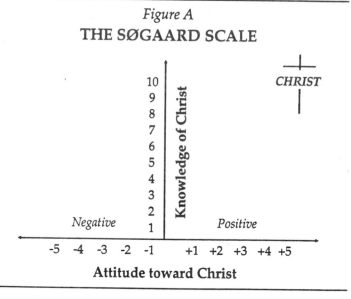

Attitude toward Christ

As Christian workers, whether in evangelism or development work, our ultimate goal is to bring our target group to the experience of Christ and the blessings of Kingdom living. The group's knowledge of Christ and their attitude towards what they know are crucial factors determining both the present position of the community in relationship to His Kingdom and whether they will ever arrive at its door.

Through research procedures described earlier and in Part Two, we can come to understand where our group fits on the scale. We can then envision a process of ministry that will both increase their knowledge of Christ and create a more positive attitude towards what they know of Him. If, for example, our target community is an extremely resistant group, we might portray their position as in Figure B. Their knowledge of the gospel is minimal, both due to illiteracy and antagonistic religious teaching.

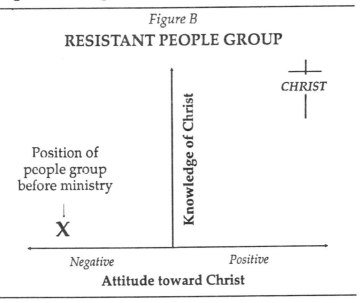

Figure B

RESISTANT PEOPLE GROUP

During the course of our investigation of this community (using the same example), we might discover that, due to severe drought in the region, their greatest need is for easily accessible water. Their women and children are spending hours each day hauling water from one of the last remaining sources of surface water. Obviously, if we as Christian workers can help this community get a well drilled, their attitude towards Christianity will be changed, becoming less negative. (Such a shift in attitude, even in groups with prior resistance to the gospel, has often been the result of Christian relief and development efforts.)

We may not have much opportunity at this stage to proclaim the gospel verbally, but we can assuredly know that definite progress will be made in this community's movement towards Christ. We can envision this progress on the Søgaard Scale in Figure C.

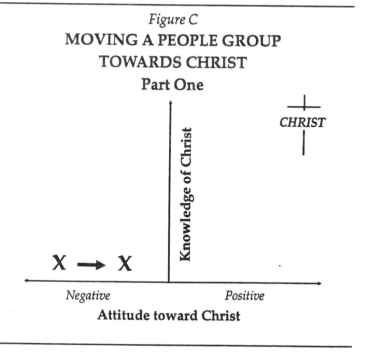

Figure C

MOVING A PEOPLE GROUP TOWARDS CHRIST

Part One

In cooperation with a church in a neighboring community, we plan to institute a literacy project for adults. This will further confirm in the minds of the group the loving concern of Christians, breaking down more prejudice and building a favorable attitude toward the sponsoring church. It will also prepare them to read the Scriptures we plan to distribute to deepen their knowledge of the Savior. Our strategy for moving the group further along towards Christ can be pictured (see Figure D) as positive movement in both vertical (knowledge) and horizontal (attitude) directions.

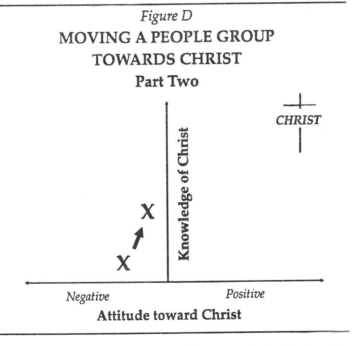

Figure D

MOVING A PEOPLE GROUP
TOWARDS CHRIST

Part Two

CHRIST

Knowledge of Christ

X

X

Negative   Positive

Attitude toward Christ

Just as the right mixture of gas and air ignite the combustion that drives an engine, so actual conversion to Christ occurs when the Holy Spirit utilizes the optimum mix of adequate knowledge and positive attitude to prompt the hearts of the people to respond to His wooing. Both our holistic strategizing coupled with the Spirit's energizing are used by God to bring the community to faith and fullness of Kingdom living.

Figure E

MOVING A PEOPLE GROUP
TOWARDS CHRIST
Part Three

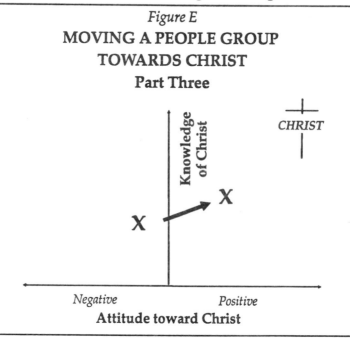

Attitude toward Christ

The Søgaard Scale may thus be used to plan a sequence of ministry efforts that enable us to see visually and maintain the appropriate relationship between evangelism and social responsibility at each stage of a people group's Kingdom odyssey. We do not need to feel guilty about stressing one more than the other for a time, knowing that we do so as part of an integrated, long-range strategy that will leave neither out over the long run and that God will ultimately use to reveal His son. We know that each sequence is just as valuable because it serves our overall purpose of moving the group towards the final destination -- redemption and participation in the Kingdom.

By utilizing a tool like the Søgaard Scale, we keep the purpose of our ministry clearly defined and before us so as not to lose sight of it in the distraction of intervening activities. We are also now in a better position to set measurable goals for our ministry for each stage of the group's journey. Measurable goals keep us on track towards achieving our purpose and give us a means of holding ourselves and others accountable for our ministry. We can then better coordinate with the efforts of other agencies and churches so all can better see where they fit in the whole process (see Figure F).

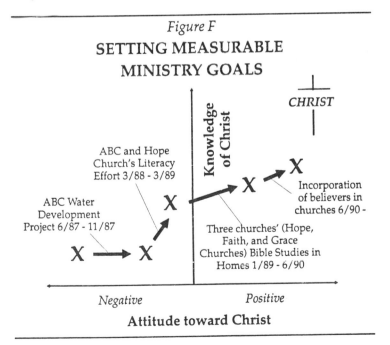

Figure F
SETTING MEASURABLE MINISTRY GOALS

This diagram will need to be redrawn periodically as conditions change and progress is made. But each time we do so, it is an opportunity to communicate with others where we see our respective roles and plans in relationship to one another, fitting together in a way that God can use ultimately to bring our intended group to Christ.

EXERCISE

Think of the group you are intending to reach. Where would you plot their present position on their Kingdom journey? Now develop a sequenced ministry strategy that will both meet their needs and take them towards the Kingdom. The following sets of axes are for this purpose.

Name of People Group:

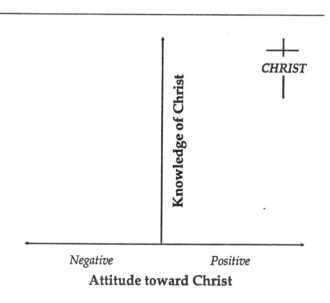

Attitude toward Christ

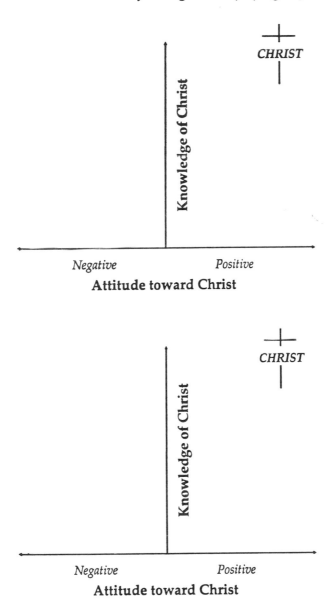

Setting ministry goals

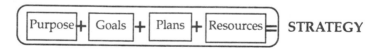

Purpose **+** Goals **+** Plans **+** Resources **=** STRATEGY

You have just had the experience of thinking through a process you and other Christian workers might employ to move your people group further along towards Christ's Kingdom. You now need to think through how you will put this strategy into operation. Often we fail to achieve our purpose in ministry because we do not pin ourselves down in writing beforehand.

Missionaries and evangelists frequently have a vague, general purpose in mind. For example, "to bring God's word to this nation" or "to reach this city for Christ." But unless a purpose is clearly defined and operationalized through measurable goals and practical plans of action, it remains nothing more than a pious wish or a noble intention.

An effective strategy is therefore composed of a clearly defined purpose, measurable goals, marking progress toward fulfillment of that purpose, and practical action plans as to how we will go about attaining our goals to make accomplishment of the overall purpose possible. We will also need to consider what resources, both human and material, will be necessary and how we will go about finding and utilizing them.

Below is an example of how we might define our purpose, set measurable goals, design practical action plans, and target utilizable resources to reach the Tuareg people of the Sahara.

Our PURPOSE is:

To establish a cell of believers among the Muslim Tuareg people of the Sahara in North Mali.

Our GOALS to achieve this PURPOSE are:

- Learn to ride a camel! (August 1989)
- Speak the Tuareg language. (April 1990)
- Using a grant from the ABC Development Agency, replace livestock lost during the recent drought. (May 1990)
- Develop friendships with one nomadic group. (June 1990)
- Understand their way of looking at the world and felt needs. (December 1990)
- Share the gospel message with ten families. (January 1991)
- Establish a Bible study group. (March 1991)
- See a cell of 20 believers meeting regularly for worship and fellowship. (June 1991)

Notice how all of these goals are measurable by time and quantity. In this way we have clarified exactly what we plan to do and can monitor whether we are accomplishing our goals effectively. Such goals keep us on track and help us hold ourselves accountable for the accomplishment of our overall purpose.

Measurable goals also give us an incentive to prayer and dependence on God. Without Him we would be unable to realize our purpose. Yet it is amazing how God works when we clarify our exact goals and turn them into prayer. Clearly it is His will for this people group to be reached, and He will guide us in the outworking and implementation of our goals, possibly modifying and changing our direction in the process. Remember Proverbs 16:9 and Paul's Macedonian experience. We need both to strategize with our God-given minds and also allow Him to lead us as we turn these goals into prayer.

Our action plans would concern the details of how we plan to accomplish our goals by the proposed date. What would two practical plans of action look like that correspond to goals one and two above?

Our plans of ACTION to accomplish these GOALS are:

- Hire Ahmad, the camel driver, to give riding lessons twice a week for the next six weeks.
- Buy Tuareg tapes and listen to them for two hours daily.
- Enroll in the North African Language Institute for classes three times a week.

Other practical plans of action could be developed for each of the goals we have outlined above. How might we find and allocate resources to carry out our strategy for the Tuareg?

RESOURCES that will be needed are:

- Other Christian workers:
  ABC development workers & two lay evangelists from Grace Church.
- Material:
  $5,000 grant for livestock replacement from ABC Development Organization Camel to be donated by Grace Church. Fees for language study and personal support totalling $5,000 per year for the

next three years (Ask Hope Church
Board for their assistance).

Now, let us give you the opportunity to go through
the same process for the people group you have determined to reach. In a sentence or two, clearly define the
purpose of your ministry. What do you expect to
achieve, say in the next five years? It is this overall
purpose that you want to keep in mind always. It should
spring from the vision of your heart for this people
group.

My PURPOSE is:

_____

_____

_____

_____

_____

_____

_____

As you contemplate that purpose, imagine what are
the stepping stones that will take you toward its fulfillment. What will you have to do first, second, third, and
so on, to achieve that ministry purpose? Now include
dates and quantities wherever it is possible so that it may
became a concrete, tangible strategy by which you and
your Christian colleagues can hold yourselves accountable.

My GOALS to achieve this PURPOSE are:

_____

_____

_____

_____

_____

_____

_____

_____

_____

_____

_____

_____

_____

_____

_____

_____

_____

_____

_____

_____

My plans of ACTION to accomplish these GOALS are:

_____

_____

_____

_____

_____

_____

_____

_____

_____

_____

_____

_____

_____

_____
_____
_____
_____
_____
_____
_____
_____
_____
_____
_____
_____
_____
_____
_____
_____
_____
_____
_____
_____
_____
_____
_____
_____
_____

RESOURCES that will be needed are:

_____
_____
_____
_____
_____
_____
_____
_____
_____

You have now had the experience of thinking through a strategy for reaching your people group on paper. In the process you may come to realize how much more you need to know about your target group. For instance, if you are going to discover their unique way of looking at the world and some particular felt needs you hope to meet during your ministry, you will need to discover that information. As you discover more about the group, that information in turn will affect your planning and the way you approach your ministry.

How can we go about getting this extra knowledge? How can we practically go about the task of researching our people group? Part Two of this book will help you. It provides some down-to-earth tools that Christian workers can use to get the information needed to guide their ministry.

Part Two

PRACTICAL PROCEDURES FOR PEOPLE GROUP THINKING

The research procedures that will be described are offered as suggestions only. You may pick and choose any that would be useful in your situation. Just as a handyman does not make use of all the tools in his bag for a particular job so you should not feel obliged to use all of them.

In this part, I have drawn together the thinking and experience of a number of field researchers besides myself, putting emphasis on those methods that could be most easily put into practice by Christian workers and which would be most applicable for Christian mission. If there is a section that does not appeal to you, go on to another. But don't get scared off by the idea of "research." It can revolutionize your ministry!

Diagram # 6

PRACTICAL PROCEDURES FOR PEOPLE GROUP THINKING

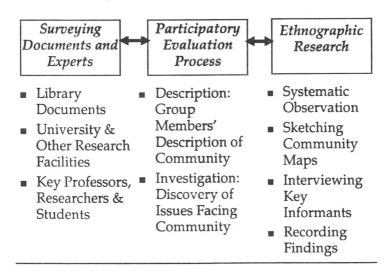

Surveying Documents and Experts	*Participatory Evaluation Process*	*Ethnographic Research*
■ Library Documents	■ Description: Group Members' Description of Community	■ Systematic Observation
■ University & Other Research Facilities		■ Sketching Community Maps
■ Key Professors, Researchers & Students	■ Investigation: Discovery of Issues Facing Community	■ Interviewing Key Informants
		■ Recording Findings

Surveying Documents and Experts

What a tragic waste of time and effort it is not to draw upon the knowledge and expertise of others. Many Christian workers plunge into ministry efforts in ignorance of valuable sources of information on their target group which are easily accessible in writing or by talking with those who already understand the group in question. They could contribute valuable insights that would help unlock the door to our target group by providing us with an entry strategy for moving into deeper research and more relevant ministry.

University libraries and other private or governmental research institutions often have a wealth of pertinent information just waiting for a curious inquirer. Just tell the librarian or curator of your interest in the particular people group you plan to investigate and ask for suggestions on relevant books, articles and other documents that may bear on the subject. He or she should be eager to assist you.

You might also ask whether he or she knows any professors, researchers or university students who have studied the group in question and whom you could interview. Sometimes anthropologists, sociologists or faculty members in other disciplines have devoted efforts in field research to the same group or a related group and could give you invaluable advice on how to proceed. They could recommend other knowledgeable people or written resources you ought to consult. They also might be able to put you in touch with key members of the target group with whom you could begin to cultivate a relationship. Be assured that God will guide you and will open up marvelous serendipities in the process.

Researching a people group is like the work of a detective looking for clues or a diver searching for sunken treasure. It is an exciting and stimulating process as one bit of information brings new enlightenment and opens up the way for other avenues of inquiry.

Surveying relevant documents and people with expertise is a good preparatory step to answering your research question -- the question you have determined is critical to the development of your ministry strategy. It is a way of looking at your target group from the outside, like peering through a window into a house.

While it is a valuable beginning and may show us how to make an initial approach to the group, we also need to get an insider perspective that only personal contact with members of the group can afford. Outside research enables us to peer into a window and even open the door, but we must actually go inside if we are to gain a clear perception of what lies within. This is the kind of inside perspective that the following procedures open up to us.

The Participatory Evaluation Process

The Participatory Evaluation Process (PEP) as utilized by World Vision* takes its inspiration from the kind of people group thinking expressed in the following poem by James Yen, one of the earliest originators of a participative approach to development.

> Go to the people
> Live among the people
> Learn from the people
> Plan with the people
> Work with the people
> Start with what the people know
> Build on what the people have...[17]

In PEP, we recognize that the people we hope to meaningfully touch for Christ are experts on themselves and their own life situation. If we want to relevantly relate the love and truth of Jesus to them, we must go as learners to live among them and learn from them. We need to listen to them describe their own reality, life as they see it with all its problems and challenges. Judy

---

* World Vision International is a Christian humanitarian organization located in Monrovia, California, with projects in over 80 countries.

Hutchinson, one of the practitioners of World Vision's PEP approach, describes the process:

> One of the lessons we have learned is that the community knows very well who they are as well as what their needs and problems are. But we have to be able to get to the level of the community and share sufficiently with them to give them trust to bring out who they are and what their needs are.[18]

In order to bring out who the members of our people group are and discern their real needs, PEP advocates two phases of learning with the people: description and investigation.

Description

After establishing sufficient rapport with various members of the community, gather as many of them as possible together for a session of self-description. Over the course of a couple of hours, using large sheets of paper and marker pens, ask them to cooperate in drawing a picture or map of their community. All should be encouraged to participate in featuring dwellings, roads, paths, wells, gardens, temples, shrines -- whatever is significant to them about their life in that place.

After the corporate drawing is finished, ask them to describe orally what they have drawn and why they have depicted things as they have. This should provoke a lively discussion. Do not dominate, but facilitate the process. Ask questions and let the people talk freely. All of you will learn volumes as they talk back and forth among themselves -- affirming and contradicting what has been said and drawn. In Ed Dayton's *That Everyone May Hear: Workbook*, produced by MARC, you will find a variety of questions that can be introduced opportunely as the discussion flows along. [19]

The completed picture can be affixed prominently to a nearby wall so all can refer to it as the session progresses. During this description phase, what we are striving to do is to understand characteristics of the people and the place in which they live.

Investigation

During the second phase of learning, you investigate along with community members the nature of the problems and needs that confront them. What do they want to change about their life situation? Perhaps the community hygiene needs to be improved -- a better garbage disposal system must be worked out and latrines provided. Perhaps you will discover they are living in fear of a certain spirit or are oppressed by absentee landlords. In an inner city neighborhood the prevalence and fear of crime may require helping to create some sort of crime prevention scheme.

Any felt needs of this kind are an entree into holistic ministry. Our integrity as those who represent Christ demands our willingness to join in their struggle for a better life.

In order to determine which problems are the most pressing, members of the people group should be encouraged to carry out their own research project. If sufficient interest and concern are generated by the discussion, they can devise a list of questions to ask others in the community to find out how the group as a whole feels. In this way, we ensure greater participation on their part in rectifying the problems that are identified. We also are letting them take charge of their own destiny rather than paternalistically doing what we think is good for them. Their dignity as creatures of God and fellow human beings is upheld.

From this process we come away with a deeper understanding of the people group *and* solid relationships of
love and caring through which the gospel can flow with
real relevance and effect. A ministry strategy will naturally begin to emerge that is not imposed upon the group
from the outside but arises from the inside. It will be
appropriate rather than forced and will meet actual
needs rather than just perceived ones. [20]

The Ethnographic Approach

Anthropologists use what is called the "ethnographic approach" to come to understand a specific people group. This approach is somewhat parallel to PEP yet provides us with extra tools to gain a deeper understanding. We can utilize both procedures complementarily as we move into a community to serve them with the gospel.

Ethnography is the study of the culture of a particular group of people and the description of that culture usually in written form. The goal of ethnography is to "grasp the native's point of view, his relation to life, to realize his vision of his world."[21]

Using this approach, we adopt the role of learners and let the members of the group in which we are interested teach us about life as they see it. In this way it is similar to PEP. We need to start with a frank admission of ignorance about our target group so that we will be completely open to what they will reveal to us about their peculiar way of perceiving reality. We must learn to listen, ask questions and listen, listen, listen some more.

As one anthropologist puts it, ethnography is a lot like cryptography, the deciphering of codes. The idea is to observe, listen and probe enough so that the investigator will be able to understand the hidden meanings behind what he sees and hears. The realm of a group's cultural knowledge is like a vast iceberg below the surface tip of its outward behavior in the world.[22]

Much of this knowledge is assumed or tacitly held by group members as insiders. Therefore, we will need to probe and make inferences from what we observe them doing and hear them saying. Gradually, as we immerse ourselves in the life of the group and document our findings, a "cultural map" will begin to take shape in our minds and on our note pads — a map that reflects the patterns by which that people group orders its life; a map that will eventually take us and others with the gospel to the very threshold of their hearts.

There are a number of field techniques that will enable us to produce such a cultural map from which strategies of ministry can be developed. You will have the opportunity to employ some of these techniques during the recommended exercises that follow.

Systematic observation

The first and most fundamental means of gathering data on a people group is through systematic observation. We can learn a lot about a group by watching them in a variety of life situations, noting their actions, reactions, and interactions, socially and individually. Observation is an essential part of scientific investigation. In the scientific method, hypotheses or hunches are deduced, tested by observation and reformulated into theories according to the evidence uncovered. In the same way, careful, repeated observation will confirm or overthrow the inferences we have developed about the culture of our people group.

One of the most simple, practical ways you can begin researching a people group is to choose one social situation such as a street scene, restaurant, provision shop, religious ritual or any other situation that is accessible to you and where you can remain fairly unobtrusive. Observe what is happening with the people, objects and events in that situation.

One social researcher advises us to ask ourselves, "What is going on here both above and below the surface in people's interactions with one another?" What unspoken cultural rules are operating that you can detect from observing their behavior and speech?[23] Write down your observations of what is happening and your inferences as to why people are behaving as they do. Do it at the same time or immediately afterwards, while it is fresh in your mind. Then move to another social situation and repeat the process.

Direct observation followed by interviewing someone who can answer questions that emerge from your study is a good way of checking your inferences. (e.g., Why did the priest make that particular gesture at that point in the ceremony? What is the meaning of that part of the ritual?) Observation, therefore, provides a helpful starting point for uncovering those questions you need to ask during later interviews with informants.

Observation also enables us to check whether informants are presenting you with an idealistic version of life or their actual practice. One social surveyor in an Indian village was told that the Brahmins were priests and the Chamars were leather workers. However, through his own observation he noticed that both groups were actually farmers most of the time. The Brahmins only gave occasional attention to the conduct of ceremonies.[24] People have a natural tendency to present their ideals as if they were actual practice. That is why perceptive observation will be fundamental to all other field procedures you employ.

EXERCISE

Begin observing the members of your intended group, watching for clues to the unique ways they look at life. Write down your observations and unanswered questions. Be insatiably curious about why people act as they do. Make a list of several social situations in which you could carry out on-site observation of your people group.

_____
_____
_____
_____
_____
_____
_____
_____
_____
_____
_____
_____
_____
_____
_____
_____
_____
_____
_____
_____
_____
_____
_____
_____

Sketching community maps

Where it is not politic or possible to initiate PEP, drawing our own topographical maps of a community's areas of residence, business centers, communications network, as well as cultural and religious institutions, can aid your understanding of their particular life situation. Talking with several informants individually about the significance of the various places depicted and preferably getting their help in completing the original drawing, can open up further realms of insight into what it is like being a member of this group.

Interviewing key informants

Interviewing members of the group is the prime means of acquiring in-depth knowledge of that group's world view, values and attitudes. As one anthropologist puts it, an interview makes it possible for the person interviewed "to bring the interviewer into his or her world."[25] If you contact a cross-section of group members representing various perspectives, a composite map of that group's culture will begin to take shape in our understanding.

There may be value in using quantitative survey approaches in which an interviewer approaches a people group with the same pre-designed, "check the blank" type of questionnaire for everyone. This type of statistical analysis approach is often used for surveying a large number of people more superficially, but it does not permit either the flexibility or in-depth probing necessary for our research purpose. Not only does this approach cut off the possibility of new unexpected information appearing, but it forces the respondents to fit their feelings and experience into the researcher's categories. This can produce distortion of what they have actually felt or experienced due to the circumscribed kinds of responses being solicited.[26]

If we genuinely want to uncover the way our target group perceives the world, it makes better sense to adopt the more qualitative approach of interviewing key informants. As one experienced research interviewer affirms: "The fundamental principle of qualitative interviewing is to provide a framework within which respondents can express their own understandings *in their own terms*" (emphasis mine).[27]

Advantages of informant interviewing

There are a number of advantages to this technique. First, in the course of surveying literature written concerning the group and of observing it firsthand, questions needing further clarification will naturally arise in our minds. We can then identify informants within the group who have specialized knowledge concerning the matters about which we are seeking explanation. For example, if you want to understand some aspect of their religious beliefs and practices, we can interview a priest, or if we want to find out more about local folk medical practices, we can interview a doctor or a traditional herbalist.

Another advantage is that we can assess not only the information conveyed orally, but also the feelings and reactions of those interviewed. How does the respondent react when we take such a line of questioning? Is he or she evasive or forthcoming, embarrassed and defensive, or frank and eager to talk? What clues to the underlying cultural framework does he or she reveal through body language, emotions expressed or suppressed, or attitudes manifested towards you as an outsider?

Interviewing individuals gives us a laboratory for firsthand observation of the group in microcosm. Each person interviewed represents the larger group in substantial ways. And as we come to understand that one part, our understanding of the whole will be enriched.

A third advantage of key informant interviewing is the opportunity it affords not only to probe for greater clarification of prior questions, but to open up whole new lines of inquiry as the interview progresses. New aspects of the culture may be brought to light as the informant is given free rein to voice his inner thoughts and feelings. This is particularly so when the interviewer has managed to establish some degree of rapport and friendship with the informant. In this situation, informant interviewing permits the curious investigator the flexibility to switch gears and pursue other intriguing questions that arise.

Cautions about informant interviewing

There are certain cautions we need to be aware of in relying on informant interviewing, however. First, we must be aware of over-generalizing our findings to the entire population. Even if we have taken pains to interview people of several different social levels and perspectives, we are still, in fact, only talking with a few representatives of the whole society. Therefore, we must avoid making sweeping statements such as, "All members of this group feel this way." It is more accurate to mention those kinds of people interviewed and say, "Those interviewed feel this way."

Another caution we need to keep in mind is the danger of bias. There are a number of types of bias that can affect the interview process. The respondent may not want to offend his honored guest and so will only respond with socially acceptable answers. This has been termed "courtesy bias." "Self-lifting bias" results in answers that enhance the image of the informant in the eyes of the interviewer. Fear is another motive that may enter into the responses of the interviewee. He or she may be afraid you will report the interview to the government or police.[28]

Being patient with your respondents until greater rapport develops and they become convinced of your credibility will help. Also, it is possible to check the answers of informants against one another to identify where bias has crept in.

Perhaps the greatest danger of bias, however, springs from our own tendency to ethnocentricism -- judging the culture of another group by our own cultural standards. As much as possible, guard against this ever present human tendency. We must endeavor to put aside our preconceptions and maintain an utter humility, openness and a desire to learn. We will have to be careful about jumping to conclusions, thinking we understand when we probably only have a vague, inaccurate idea of what is going on.

Native Americans have an apt proverb which goes something like this: I will not judge another person until I have walked in his moccasins. In the same way, we cannot avoid the distortion of ethnocentric bias until we have lived with a people group, humbly listening and learning for a considerable length of time. Isn't it a point to ponder that Jesus spent thirty years learning the ways of the Aramaic-speaking Galileans before beginning to preach the gospel to them for only three years? By now it becomes obvious that this kind of work takes patience and time. But it is well worth it!

After recognizing and seeking to avoid the dangers of bias and ethnocentricism, we must develop several skills essential to a successful interview with a key informant.

Finding good informants

In order to acquire good information on our people group, we need to have access to good informants. We ought to be making this a matter of prayer throughout the time of our investigation, asking God to guide us to the right individuals or families that would be willing to give of their time, and share their wisdom with us. We can trust God to lead us and give us His discernment throughout the whole interviewing process, as well as His favor in building rapport with our informants.

What makes a good informant? First, he or she should know the culture of the group intimately. In other words, the person should be part of the cultural mainstream and not a new arrival or outsider undergoing assimilation into the group. Furthermore, it is best if informants have direct experience and knowledge of the particular matter you are interested in investigating.

Local professionals like doctors, teachers, nurses, civil servants, social workers, and others whose occupations bring them into contact with a wide range of individuals, make good informants.[29] Coffee shop owners and barbers are other strong candidates, due to their extensive clienteles and the kind of relaxed social interaction that often takes place on their premises.[30]

As mentioned before, informants should be selected so as to represent different factions and points of view within the community. That means interviewing not just the erudite and rich elite, but also the illiterate, poor and marginalized.

A good way to build up a list of additional potential informants is after each interview to ask the person being consulted for the names of one or two others who would be knowledgeable about the matter under scrutiny.

Building rapport

Establishing rapport with those we want to interview is a critical ingredient in the whole process. Unless we are successful in this, our informants will not feel comfortable enough to speak freely. After all, they may suspect we are tax collectors or policemen. We therefore should not rush into asking questions until we have sufficiently introduced ourselves and the reason for which we have come.

We can be honest and forthright about our purpose without revealing everything we hope to do with the information sought. We might, for example, introduce ourselves as members of a local church interested in developing programs that will be of greater service to that community, or as someone who is doing research on culture. There may be other ways to be introduced that will allay suspicion about our intentions and get them to talk. Remember, we have nothing to hide. Our intention is to be of real service to that group in Christ's name.

Another means of gaining rapport is showing unfeigned interest in their culture. People generally like to talk about themselves and what is precious to them, if they are assured of another's genuine interest and respect.

Other suggestions are:

- Begin the interviews with subjects that are less threatening, being sensitive about the proper

timing and way in which to probe more
deeply.

- Learn and follow local customs and etiquette
  as much as possible.
- Do not make comparisons of the local culture
  with your own.
- Do not stay longer than what was agreed on
  for the interview time.
- Maintain the confidences of your informants,
  keeping their identities to yourself.[31]

EXERCISE

Prepare a list of potential informants. Identify particular
kinds of bias likely to enter into your interviews with
them. How do you plan to build rapport? What field
procedures do you think will be most beneficial in your
situation?

_____

_____

_____

_____

_____

_____

_____

_____

_____

_____

_____

_____

_____

_____

_____

_____

_____

_____

_____

_____

_____

_____

_____

_____

_____

_____

_____

_____

_____

Interviewing styles

There are essentially two styles of interviewing. The first is to let the conversation take its own course and let questions arise spontaneously as the verbal interchange proceeds. In this style, it is possible the informant may not even be aware that he or she is being interviewed. Indeed, we may adopt this style to listen to members of the group carrying on their own conversations in public places like restaurants, on buses or trains, or during a haircut at the local barber's. The idea in either case is to listen for the issues they themselves raise and about which they have the strongest feelings. What are they worried, happy, sad, angry, fearful, or hopeful about? Development specialists term this activity "listening for generative themes", themes of strong enough concern to the community that they will generate sufficient drive to break through group apathy and ignite corporate initiative to overcome their obstacles.[32]

As Christian workers, an awareness of such generative themes will enable us to proceed directly to addressing these issues pertinently and powerfully in the way we communicate the gospel and to demonstrate Christ's love through practical caring about those matters that mean most to those we are endeavoring to reach.

In this style, the interviewer assumes a passive stance, allowing the interviewee to ramble on at will. He or she does not attempt to order the interview or make it conform to his agenda. Disadvantages are the larger amount of time required to discover what you want to know, and your lack of control of the interview.

A second, contrasting style is coming to an interview with a mental or written list of questions you would like answered and assertively guiding the session with this purpose in mind.

The strength of this approach is keeping communication focused on the particular subjects of your interest, while allowing the flexibility to diverge if you think it is worthwhile. Prepare several questions beforehand and endeavor to maintain enough control over the conversation to get them answered.

The challenge in utilizing this style is balancing the need to be sensitive to the respondent's feelings with the need to cover the items on your agenda. Using both styles is recommended: the first during times of systematic observation when you are delving for issues and questions to bring up with your informant, the second when you need to get such questions answered.

Asking effective questions

How do we go about asking effective questions, questions that will function as keys to unlocking our informant's warehouse of cultural knowledge? Asking good questions is akin to a form of art.

Ambiguous questions are one of the great enemies of successful interviewing. Our words need to be carefully chosen with the interviewee's perception in mind so as not to muddle his replies. Some years ago, researchers in the United States asked rural adults if they "favored government control of profits". Several responded emphatically in the negative, stating that "prophets should be regulated only by the Lord!" [33]

Loaded questions are questions in which the wording favors a certain response. For example, "Many others I have interviewed say... Would you agree or disagree?" Of course the respondents would be likely to agree with the "many others" since, in expressing their opinions, people generally tend to go along with the crowd. Loaded questions prejudice a fair and open response.

In some cases, if the subject is sensitive and you think the respondent will be reluctant to express his opinion, you can ask the question indirectly. For example, instead of saying "How do you feel about...?", you might say "How would you say your friends and relatives feel about...?" You can broaden the scope of your questions to include the whole people group by saying "How would most of your people feel about...?"

In his helpful book on ethnographic interviewing, James Spradley recommends beginning an interview with broad, overarching questions that ask the informant to describe his or her experience or knowledge of the particular phenomenon under consideration. He suggests asking "grand tour" questions, allowing the informant to provide a guided tour, or overview, of a subject. For example, "Can you describe what happens during the New Moon Festival?" Or, "Could you tell me the functions of all the participants?" [34]

Other examples of grand tour questions might be:

- "Could you describe a typical day of work at the mine?"
- "Could you describe the lifestyle of the rickshaw drivers and their families?"
- "Could you explain the significance of these places on this map?"

"Mini-tour questions," according to Spradley, are follow-up questions that explore specific areas opened up by the broader grand tour queries. For example, "Could you describe what happened during this part of the ritual?" or "Could you describe in more detail what the significance of this particular place on the map is?" In probing for additional details we can use the interrogatives who, when, what, where, how to uncover more information.[35]

In the flow of interviewing, we ordinarily move from overarching, descriptive kinds of questions to more focused, selective ones. The process may be envisaged as a funnel, moving from the general to the specific.[36]

Diagram #7

THE INTERVIEWING PROCESS

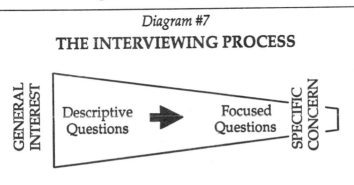

GENERAL INTEREST — Descriptive Questions → Focused Questions — SPECIFIC CONCERN

EXERCISES

What different styles of interviewing would you feel most comfortable with and which would be most suitable for your particular people group? Based on what you know and do not yet know about your people group, review the different types of questions and prepare an actual list of questions to ask your first informant.

_____

_____

_____

_____

_____

_____

_____

_____

_____

_____

_____

_____

_____

_____

_____

_____

_____

_____

_____

_____

_____

_____

_____

_____

_____

_____
_____
_____
_____
_____
_____
_____
_____
_____
_____

Recording findings

Recording the substance of your observation periods and interviews is extremely important. Notes should be taken in an abbreviated form during the sessions themselves if this does not adversely affect rapport with the informant. Otherwise, you will need to write down your recollection of what was said or what you observed immediately afterwards.

It is possible to use key words or phrases to make a condensed account that can later be amplified and written up properly. This expanded account should be completed the same day before a night's sleep blurs the exactness of your memory. Be sure to use the actual words of the respondent whenever possible. The very act of writing will sharpen your observation and reflective skills leading you on to additional questions to propose next time.

If you have achieved enough rapport with your informants, try using a tape recorder if one is available. If those you are interviewing don't mind your using one it can enable you to concentrate more carefully. If they are skittish about having certain parts of the interview recorded, you can put them at ease by agreeing to turn your recorder off whenever a sensitive matter comes up that they would object to having taped.

EXERCISES

With some specific questions in mind practice interviewing a friend or colleague. Then switch and let him/her interview you. Afterwards critique one another by giving your reaction to their questions. How could they be more sensitively and effectively phrased?

Field Exercises

The following two exercises are suggestions for beginning ethnographic research in the field.

- Observe members of your people group in two social situations. Spend one-half hour in observation for each, writing up field notes of what you observed and what inferences you draw from your observations, as well as further questions for investigation that have arisen.

- Interview one informant for one hour, or two informants for one-half hour each, using questions you have developed as a result of the earlier periods of observation. Again, write up your notes in condensed form.

Upon your return from the field, take time to write up your conclusions and share your findings with others. Discuss problems encountered and possible solutions.

_____
_____
_____
_____
_____
_____
_____
_____
_____
_____
_____
_____
_____
_____
_____
_____
_____

_____

_____

_____

_____

_____

_____

_____

_____

_____

_____

_____

_____

_____

_____

_____

_____

_____

_____

_____

_____

_____

_____

_____

_____

_____

_____

_____

_____

Sharing the Results of Your Research

People group research is meant to be shared with others who feel concern for this community and can join forces with you to touch them with the love and power of Christ. One of the most useful ways of doing this is to write up a summary of what you have learned after employing some of the field procedures described.

After spending some time surveying relevant documents, talking to experts, engaging in PEP sessions, times of systematic observation, or interviewing key informants, and of course recording your conclusions, you will be ready to write up a profile on this group that can serve as the basis for developing relevant ministries.

At this stage, take out all your notes and go through them looking for patterns that emerge. Fitting all the pieces of information together will feel something like assembling a jigsaw puzzle, but as you do it, a clear cultural portrait of the group should emerge. Perhaps you will discover missing pieces during the process. If so, you may need to go back to your informants with another list of questions. Do not leave any stone unturned in ferreting out significant information.

In writing your profile, wherever possible, provide concrete illustrations or actual quotations to substantiate and add color to your generalizations. Besides corroborating your conclusions, such real life anecdotes will make your profile more realistic and compelling to those who read it.

Another effective way of communicating the results of your research you might consider is preparing a short audio-visual. You can take your notes or completed profile and turn them into a narrative with accompanying slides. Many presentations of this sort have left a life-changing impact on their audiences, moving believers to get involved in reaching particular groups they had been oblivious to before.

In Malaysia, some of my national colleagues and I took the research we had done and prepared an audio-visual on local people groups that has stirred many young people to consider going as missionaries to the unreached. You cannot reach your target group alone. Your job as one whose research has made you an expert is to communicate the vision to others who can work with you to minister to them.

Finally, in the process of sharing your research findings with others, follow Jesus' injunction to "pray the Lord of the harvest, that he will send forth laborers" into this section of His harvest (Matthew 9:36-38). It is the experience of many who have been involved in advocating the cause of needy and unreached peoples, that God will do this as we pray specifically and continually. Make your informants, research findings, and the people group as a whole the focus of fervent, ongoing prayer, and you will see the Lord begin to work His wonders. He will raise up gifted workers to partner with you in your ministry effort.

Decide how and with whom you will share your research findings. What outcomes do you foresee? Resolve to spend regular time in prayer for your target group. Find others who can join you in caring, praying and going to this group with the Good News of Christ.

Part Three

RELEASING GOD'S POWER THROUGH PRAYER

Prayer Releases God's Power for Mission to the Unreached

Today's hyperactive Christian workers often treat prayer more as a harmless pastime rather than a powerful resource. We pray routinely as we open and close meetings, say grace at the table, or as a special consolation in time of emergency or stress. In our attitude we often relegate prayer to those who are retired or who "have nothing better to do with their time." Certainly for most mission leaders, prayer does not seem to be where the action is; otherwise, wouldn't we give it far more attention in our lives?

A Revealing Case Study

One of the greatest illustrations of prayer as a powerful resource in frontier missions is found in the experience of J.O. Fraser, the pioneer missionary to the Lisu tribe of southwest China. As a young missionary with the China Inland Mission in the early 1900s, he preached Christ for several years among the far-flung mountain villages of this people with almost no outward results. Fraser's few converts fell back into the clutches of demonism, and he himself, attacked by severe depression and suicidal despair, almost gave up his mission. Breakthrough occurred when two things happened:

- The Spirit of God enabled him to pray "the prayer of faith" for several hundred Lisu families to come to Christ.

- He succeeded in forming a prayer support group of eight to ten Christians in his home country to back up the work in ongoing prayer.

His wife later wrote about the difference this prayer effort made in Fraser's work:

> He described to me how in his early years he had been all but defeated by the forces of darkness arrayed against him.... He came to the place where he asked God to take away his life rather than allow him to labor on without results. He would then tell me of the prayer forces that took up the burden at home and the tremendous lifting of the cloud over his soul, of the gift of faith that was given him and how God seemed suddenly to step in, drive back the forces of darkness and take the field.[37]

---

*World evangelization is
an issue to be decided
by spiritual power.*

Fraser himself said:

> Work on our knees. I am feeling more and more that it is after all just the prayer of God's people that call down blessing upon the work, whether they are directly engaged in it or not. Paul may plant and Apollos water, but it is God who gives the increase, and this increase can be brought

down from heaven by believing prayer whether offered in China or in England.... If this is so, then Christians at home can do as much for foreign missions as those actually on the field. I believe it will only be known on the last day how much has been accomplished in missionary work by the prayers of earnest believers at home...

Solid lasting missionary work is done on our knees. What I covet more than anything else is earnest believing prayer, and I write to ask you to continue in prayer for me and the work here.[38]

I used to think that prayer should have the first place and teaching the second. I now feel that it would be truer to give prayer the first, second and third places and teaching the fourth.... We are not dealing with an enemy that fires at the head only—that keeps the mind only in ignorance—but with an enemy who uses poison gas attacks which wrap the people around with deadly effect and yet are impalpable, elusive... Nor would it be of any more avail to teach or preach to Lisu here while they are held back by these invisible forces... But the breath of God can blow away all those miasmic vapors from the atmosphere of a village in answer to your prayers. We are not fighting against flesh and blood. You deal with the fundamental issues of this Lisu work when you pray against the principalities, the powers, the world rulers of this darkness, the spiritual hosts of wickedness in the heavenlies (Eph. 6:12).[39]

In the years that followed hundreds of families accepted Christ, and ultimately a people movement involving tens of thousands of Lisus ensued. Today in southwest China and northern Burma they are a missionary tribe taking the gospel to other tribes about them.

Prayer: a missing link in world evangelization?

What would have happened if Fraser had not formed that prayer support group which he so faithfully kept informed with updates from the field? Would the breakthrough have occurred? In the decades since, how many potential breakthroughs among the unreached have not occurred because: 1) prayer was not perceived and used as a powerful resource, and 2) prayer supporters were not kept linked continuously to a particular unreached group or provided with a supply of up-to-date information? Could it be that prayer as perceived and practiced by "Great Commission Christians" is a crucial *missing* link in the accomplishment of world evangelization?

After dealing with the nature and importance of prayer briefly, I would like to enumerate some reasons from Scripture, history and current experience, why prayer may be the crucial link, the powerful resource in reaching unreached peoples. Having demonstrated the importance of strengthening this link, we will then put our minds together in discussion to discover new ways we might solidly link focused intercession and the unevangelized world.

Prayer at its very heart is a linking activity. First, prayer links us with God to receive His power and direction as we pray for the world and carry out our

own ministries. Second, as we pray for the unevangelized world, it links us with particular unreached
groups and the Christian workers laboring among
them. It links our efforts and their efforts to God in His
omnipotence, without whose help all such efforts ultimately are in vain.

---

*Prayer links us with God for His
power and direction. Prayer links
us with unreached groups and
Christian workers among them.*

O. Hallesby writes:

> The work of prayer is prerequisite to all other
> work in the Kingdom of God for the simple rea-
> son that it is by prayer that we *couple* [italics
> added] the powers of Heaven to our helpless-
> ness, the powers which can turn water into
> wine and remove mountains in our own life
> and the lives of others, the powers which can
> awaken those who sleep in sin and raise up the
> dead, the powers which can capture strong-
> holds and make the impossible possible.[40]

Yet having said this, prayer can often be the missing
link in our efforts on behalf of the unevangelized
world. As important as good organization, planning
and strategy are in world evangelization, in our busy-
ness for God we may have neglected to link up with
His power and direction to carry out that particular
part of His mission given to us. And that is a crucial
omission.

While doing research at a seminary library for this chapter, I was startled to discover amidst their sizeable holdings on missions no book specifically on the subject of prayer and unreached peoples. True, there were passing references to prayer in volumes on the history of missions and the theology of missions. But the great bulk of books dealt with issues of mission strategy, organization and planning. Could this unwitting omission at one of the great schools of missiology reflect a more general neglect of a critical factor in the accomplishment of world evangelization?

Every time the church has set
herself to praying there have
been stupendous movements
in the mission world.
—A.T. Pierson

In reflecting on the failure of his generation to evangelize the world by 1900, A.T. Pierson attributed the failure not only to a lack of consecration in the church evidenced by a lack of giving, faith and personal holiness, but most of all to the lack of prevailing prayer. He wrote:

Every time the church has set herself to praying there have been stupendous movements in the mission world. If we should but transfer the stress of our dependence and emphasis from appeals to men to appeals to God—from trust in organization to trust in supplication—from confidence in methods to importunate prayer for the power of the Holy Spirit, we should see results more astounding than have yet been wrought.

There is...too little simple looking unto that real source of success, the power of God in answer to prayer, first to open doors of access, then to raise up and thrust forth laborers and then to break down all opposition and make the truth mighty in converting, subduing, saving and sanctifying.[41]

Participants at the Northfield Convention of 1885 expressed the same sentiment:

But above all else our immediate and imperative need is a new spirit of earnest and prevailing prayer. The first Pentecost crowned ten days of united, continued supplication. Every subsequent advance may be directly traced to believing prayer and upon this must depend a new Pentecost. We therefore earnestly appeal to all fellow disciples to join us and each other in importunate daily supplication for a new and mighty effusion of the Holy Spirit upon all ministers, missionaries, evangelists, pastors, teachers and Christian workers and upon the whole earth; that God would impart to all Christ's witnesses the tongues of fire and melt hard hearts before the burning message. It is not by might, not by power but by the Spirit of the Lord that all true success must be secured. Let us call upon God till He answereth by fire![42]

Twenty-five years later the year 1900 had come and gone. At the conclusion of the great Edinburgh Conference on Mission in 1910, Jonathan Goforth expressed his disillusionment with the missions movement for generally failing to follow through in making prayer an ongoing priority in world evangelization:

Listening to the addresses that day one could not but conclude that the giving of the Gospel to lost mankind was largely a matter of better organization, better equipment, more men and women. Symptoms indeed were not lacking that a few more sparks might have precipitated an explosion. But no, the dethronement of the idol of ecclesiastical self-efficiency was apparently too great a price to pay.... We still refuse to face the unchangeable truth that "it is not by might nor by power, but BY MY SPIRIT."[43]

Perhaps the Edinburgh Conference Report also betrays a recognition that prayer had not been given its due in the years before and after 1900: "When the church sets itself to pray with the same seriousness and strength of purpose that it has devoted to other forms of Christian effort, it will see the Kingdom of God come with power."[44]

Whether or not prayer became a missing link in the global missions effort before and after 1900 is a question for further research. Nevertheless, we face the same danger today of falling into the trap of thinking that if we were just better organized, just better coordinated, just better deployed with our people and resources, we would be able to accomplish world evangelization.

Pierson and Goforth were right. They realized that world evangelization above all is an issue to be decided by spiritual power, the power of the Holy Spirit released in response to the prayers of His people.

Arthur Matthews, the late former missionary of the China Inland Mission, put his finger on the reason that we often do not emphasize prayer enough:

> The concept that treats prayer as if it were a supplemental booster in getting some project off the ground makes the project primary and the prayer secondary. Prayer was never meant to be incidental to the work of God. It is the work.[45]

Nine compelling reasons to pray

Could we and other missions strategists be guilty of treating prayer as if it were a nice add-on to the other "strategic" things we are doing? Could it be that we have ignored the most strategic activity in accomplishing world evangelization? Nine reasons from Scripture, the history of missions and current missionary experience all compel us to contend that prayer is our most powerful resource in frontier missions.

1. God desires and requires intercessory prayer for the accomplishment of His saving purpose for the peoples of the earth.

Jesus told us to pray, "Thy will be done on earth as it is done in Heaven." Abraham interceded for Lot in Sodom, Moses prayed that God would turn from His wrath against Israel, Daniel for the return of Israel from Babylon. Ezekiel was told by God, "I looked for a man among them who would build up the wall and stand before me in the gap on behalf of the land so I would not have to destroy it but I found none" (Ez. 22:30).

*God requires prayer for accomplishing
His purpose for the peoples of the earth*

Why does God desire and require His people's intercession? Most likely because God originally gave dominion of the earth to humankind. That dominion has never been revoked by God. Satan's dominion achieved through rebellion against the Creator is a false, illegitimate, usurped dominion. Redeemed through Christ, we can exercise our God-given right to influence the affairs of this world through the exercise of intercessory prayer. Like Kuwait's request for the multi-national force to come against the illegitimate dominion of Iraq, so we in prayer as God's redeemed children, pray that His will be done, His kingdom come on earth. Prayer in the power of the Holy Spirit breaks through the false dominion of the enemy, and clears the way for His deliverance and shalom to come to all peoples. Linked through prayer with the risen Christ, sitting at His side (Eph.2) far above all authority and dominion, we share in the accomplishment of His redemptive purposes.

Dick Eastman, president of World Literature Crusade, told our staff at World Vision that early in 1988 God had led him to take a team of intercessors throughout Eastern Europe. Their mission was "to confront the strongholds of Communism." In obedience to God's leading, they carried out a "prayer walk" around the Politbureau building in Bucharest where less than two years later, Ceaucescu made his last stand after pridefully announcing his regime would last for a thousand years. While in Berlin, God led Dick to go out with a German friend in the middle of the night to face that still forbidding wall. Moved in intercessory prayer, they both laid their hands on the wall and prayed, "In the name of Jesus, come down!"

In the dramatic events of 1989 in Eastern Europe, God used the prayers of His people to shake the nations. He can do the same thing in the unevangelized world. He is seeking those who will stand before him in the gap for the 2,000 major unreached peoples, the 1,000 unevangelized cities, and the 30 unevangelized countries.

2. Victory in the spiritual realm is primary, and it is won by prayer.

Remember Moses' intercession as he held up his hands before God while Joshua and the army of Israel fought the Amalekites in the valley below? Each time Moses' arms grew tired and faltered, Israel's army was pushed back. But as he sustained his stance in prayer with uplifted arms, the Israelites were victorious.

Later in Israel's history, King Jehoshaphat relied on the weapons of united fasting and prayer, public worship and praise which brought God's intervention against the invading armies of Israel's enemies. Bible teacher Derek Prince writes:

> These weapons, scripturally employed by Christians today, will gain victories as powerful and dramatic as they gained for the people of Judah in the days of Jehoshaphat.... Victory in the spiritual realm is primary. It is to be obtained by spiritual weapons. Thereafter its outcome will be manifested in every area of the natural and material realm.[46]

These two biblical episodes vividly portray intercessory prayer as the winning factor. Why should this be any different in today's battle for world evangelization?

3. Prayer has always undergirded and extended the missionary outreach of the church.

Prayer is mentioned over 30 times in the Book of Acts alone, and generally it is mentioned as occurring just before major breakthroughs in the outward expansion of the early Christian movement. For the Apostles, extended times of united prayer and waiting on God together were pivotal in their mission to the unreached.

Moses intercedes

Before the first great outpouring of the Spirit at Pentecost and Peter's mighty sermon that brought 3,000 into the church, it is recorded that the Apostles "all joined together constantly in prayer" (Acts 1:14). Then, as the Apostles and their new converts "devoted themselves to prayer," signs and wonders occurred, the city was filled with awe, and people were added to the church daily (2:42-44). It was "after they had prayed" that the place where they were meeting was shaken, all were filled with the Holy Spirit, and spoke the word of God with boldness (4:31).

The Apostles early on let it be known what their priority in mission was—"We will devote ourselves to prayer and the ministry of the Word" (6:4). The result of the Apostles' determined adherence to this priority was that "The word of God spread and the number of disciples increased rapidly, and a large number of the priests became obedient to the faith" (6:7).

United prayer brings
breakthroughs in mission

Peter's prayer resulted in signs and wonders such as the raising of Tabitha. Later it was a time of prayer that opened his eyes to the revelation that the gospel was also for the Gentiles, making him willing to go and preach to Cornelius. It was also the church's prayer that brought the release of Peter from prison.

A period of prayer and fasting by five leaders of the Antioch church led to the setting apart of Paul and Barnabas for their frontier mission to the Gentiles. Afterwards they were sent out with more fasting and prayer (13:1-3). It was through prayer that Paul was not allowed by the Spirit of Jesus to enter Bithynia, but redirected into Macedonia. And it was through the prayer and praise of God by the imprisoned Paul and Silas that an earthquake helped to originate the church at Philippi!

The whole European side of the modern Protestant missionary enterprise grew out of Pietism, a revival movement that was steeped in earnest prayer. From its influence the Danish-Halle Mission to India went forth, and the Moravian movement under Count Zinzendorf emerged. One author writing about the Moravians said that "the glorious movement of the Spirit... among the Moravians at Herrnhut in 1727 [which] transformed them into what has been the mightiest evangelizing force in the world for the past two centuries, was born in prayer."[47]

The prayer meeting that the Moravians began in 1727 went on a hundred years! By relays they offered unceasing prayer for the church and needs all around the world. This prayer effort kindled their desire to proclaim Christ to the unreached and led to the beginning of modern missions. And from this one small village, over 100 missionaries went out in 25 years.

Decades later William Carey, while still employed as a humble shoe repairman to support his part-time preaching, drew a homemade map of the world, entering all information he could find about its regions and countries. As he mused over the world's appalling needs and problems, he turned the information he gathered into heartfelt intercession. His biographer reveals: "Often in the silence of the night... by the dim rush light, he would scan that map and then kneeling before it, pour out his soul to God."[48] Prayer for the world was a definite motive force in the call and service of the one who came to be known as "the father of modern Protestant missions."

In 1806, a few college students from Williams College took refuge from a sudden rainstorm beneath a haystack. Sitting in the midst of hay, they used the time to pray for the world and its needs. Out of that unlikely venue for a prayer meeting, the American mission movement was born.

Robert Glover sums up the role of prayer in the history of missions:

> From Pentecost and the Apostle Paul, right down through the centuries to the present day, the story of missions has been the story of answered prayer. Every fresh outbreak of missionary energy has been the result of believing prayer. Every new missionary undertaking that has been owned and blessed of God has been

the germinating of seed planted by the divine spirit in the hearts of praying saints.[49]

4. Spiritual revivals wrought by prayer have had a major impact on frontier missions.

It has been said that "all the mighty spiritual revivals which constitute the mountain peaks of missionary annals had their roots in prayer."[50] Jonathan Goforth, missionary revivalist in Asia at the beginning of this century, described the powerful revivals and awakenings that took place in Korea and China, which not only revived the church but also brought tens of thousands of unreached peoples to Christ. It all began with small bands of believers deciding to pray together regularly for an outpouring of God's Spirit upon them and upon the unconverted. Goforth later discovered it was not only the missionaries who had been praying, but someone in his home country:

> When I came to England, I met a certain saint of God. We talked about the revival in China and she gave me certain dates when God specially pressed her to pray. I was almost startled on looking up these dates to find that they were the very dates when God was doing his mightiest work in Manchuria and China.... I believe the day will come when the whole inward history of that revival will be unveiled and will show that it was not the one who speaks to you now, but some of God's saints hidden away with Him in prayer who did most to bring it about. [51]

In Hawaii, the revival known as the "Great Awakening" (1837-43) began in the hearts of missionaries who were moved strongly to pray. At their annual meetings in 1835 and 1836 "they were powerfully moved to pray and were so deeply impressed with the need of an outpouring of the Spirit that they prepared a strong appeal to the home churches, urging Christians everywhere to unite with them in prayer for a baptism on high."[52] There were soon signs of growing interest in spiritual things among non-Christians, and then in 1837, so sweeping a spiritual awakening occurred that the missionaries had to labor night and day to accommodate multitudes anxiously seeking the assurance of salvation. In one day over 1,700 converts were baptized and in six years, 27,000 were added to the church.

J. Edwin Orr, the late historian of revivals, observed that the 19th century spiritual awakenings "revived all the existing missionary societies and enabled them to enter other fields... [and] practically every missionary invasion was launched by men revived or converted in the awakenings."[53] Of four great outpourings of the Holy Spirit in the 19th century, he wrote:

> The turn of the century awakenings sent off pioneer missionaries to the South Seas, to Latin America, Black Africa, India and China. There arose denominational missionary societies such as the Baptist Missionary Society, the American Board, and other national missions in Europe.... Then a second wave of revival reinforced the foreign missionary invasion of all the continents.... William Carey was followed by societies ready to evangelize India. Robert Morrison opened a way for missionaries to settle in the

treaty ports of China.... Missionaries pushed north from the Cape of Good Hope as David Livingstone explored the hinterlands of Africa.[54]

Of great importance to this study is the fact that Orr traced the origin of the spiritual awakenings which launched new missionary enterprises to worldwide prayer meetings which intensified before the awakenings occurred.

David Bryant concurs with Orr's analysis. He has detected a fivefold pattern in the outward movements of the gospel over the last 300 years:

- A movement of united prayer begins.
- A renewed vision of Christ and His church emerges.
- The church is restored in unity and in its determination to obey the lordship of Christ.
- A revitalization of existing ministries and outreach occurs.
- This leads to an expansion of the gospel among those who have been untouched to that point.

Bryant observes, "God's primary strategy is to bring his people together in prayer... in order that they might seek him unitedly. They pursue in prayer a fresh revelation of the glory of God's son so as to penetrate all levels of society with the gospel and to launch new mission thrusts to the ends of the earth."[55] He quotes J.Edwin Orr: "Whenever God is ready to do a new thing with his people he always sets them apraying!"

5. Intercessory prayer enables God's children to possess their inheritance, the peoples of the earth.

In Psalm 2:8 the Lord invites us as His children to "Ask of me and I will make the nations your inheritance and the ends of the earth your possession." The only thing we can take with us into eternity as our inheritance are other people. Our joy and crown, just as they were for Paul, will be others who come to Christ through our efforts. As this Psalm reveals, asking or praying opens the door to God's making the nations, or more specifically the frontier peoples, our inheritance.

In the history of missions, great ingatherings into the church of Christ appear to be linked to strong, persistent praying. John Hyde, missionary to northern India, became known as "the apostle of prayer" since God raised up scores of national workers in answer to his prayers. He made a covenant with God to pray for one person to accept Christ each day, which resulted in 400 conversions the first year. The following year, he decided to trust God for two a day, with 800 coming to Christ that year. Finally, the next year, as his faith grew, he trusted God for four a day. Through much travail in prayer, four a day came to Christ through his work.[56]

A woman missionary influenced by Hyde's prayer life resolved to devote the best hours of her time to prayer, making prayer primary and not secondary as before. God said to her, "Call upon me and I will show thee great and mighty things. You have not called upon me and therefore you do not see these things in your work." As she began to make prayer the priority in her ministry, enormous changes resulted with 15 baptized at first, and 125 adults coming to Christ during the first half of the following year. Later she wrote, "Our Christians now number 600 in contrast with one-sixth of that number two years ago."[57]

In India, prayer also proved to be the key to great ingatherings among unreached peoples. Missionaries working among the Telugu outcastes were discouraged almost to the point of abandoning the work because of the lack of response. However, on the last night of 1853, a missionary couple and three Indian helpers spent the night in prayer for the Telugus on a hill overlooking the city of Ongole. When the first light of day dawned, they all shared a sense of assurance that their prayers had prevailed. Gradually the opposition broke over the next few years, and a mighty outpouring of the Spirit brought 8,000 Telugus to Christ in only a six-week period. In one day more than 2,200 were baptized and this church became the largest in the world![58]

In 1902, two lady missionaries with the Khassia Hills Mission were challenged by the need to pray, and Khassian Christians also began to pray for their unconverted fellows. In a few months more than 8,000 were added to the church in that section of India.[59]

Wesley Duewel of OMS International, known as a teacher on prayer for missions, told me recently that the first 25 years of their mission's work in India was very slow. On the average, only one church per year came into being. Out of a period of intense heart searching by the team of missionaries, the decision was made to recruit 1,000 people in their homelands to pray 15 minutes a day for the work. Not long afterward, things began to move substantially. Over the next several years, the mission went from 25 churches with 2,000 believers, to 550 churches with more than 73,000 believers. Duewel believes the massive amount of prayer, harnessed and specifically focused on their efforts, turned the tide. One of his Indian coworkers exclaimed to him: "All of us are seeing results beyond anything we could have imagined!"

Jonathan Goforth, writing about the Korean revival of 1907, said: "[It was] intense, believing prayer that had so much to do with the revival which... brought 50,000 Koreans to Christ. We are convinced too that all movements of the Spirit in China which have come within our own experience may be traced to prayer." One missionary remarked to him, "Since the Lord did so much with our small amount of praying, what might He not have done if we had prayed as we ought?"[60]

6. Effective mission strategies come from research immersed in prayer.

Joshua was one of the original "researchers" who spied out the land of promise in Numbers 13. Because he knew the facts about the land and its peoples so well, he was prepared to become the great military strategist during the conquest. However, in the book of Joshua, we see him continually seeking God for His guidance in the development of effective strategies. He did not lean on his own understanding, but relied upon God's direction given through prayer.

The principle is still the same. I am becoming more and more convinced that coupling research findings concerning the people group we are trying to reach with ongoing persevering prayer is an unstoppable combination in the process of developing effective mission strategy. John Dawson's recent book *Taking Our Cities for God: How to Break Spiritual Strongholds* insightfully ties together ministry-related research and intercessory prayer.

7. **Prayer is the supernatural way of multiplying and sending out Christian workers into frontier missions.**

As in the days of Jesus, the harvest is still plentiful and the workers are few. World A, the unevangelized world, still claims only a tiny portion of the missions force and the Church's material resources. We have talked about the issues of redeployment and mobilization for World A. Jesus' answer in a similar situation faced in his time is still the answer today: "Pray the Lord of the harvest to send out workers into His harvest field (Matthew 9:37-38)." Jesus did not tell the disciples to go all-out and round up as many Christian workers as possible, or to raise a million dollars for mission. Instead he said that prayer to the One who owns the harvest was the priority. God can call, equip and send those workers who will be best able to reap the harvest.

I am convinced that the mightiest missionaries to the Muslims are not even converted yet. But God is waiting upon the prayers of His people to turn Muslim zealots around as he did the Apostle Paul, so they become missionaries to their people. I am convinced that as prayer networks are formed, focusing on particular peoples, cities and countries, we will see God raise up armies of new workers to reap the harvest in World A (the unevangelized world).

In 1880, when the China Inland Mission had only 100 workers, and again in 1887, when additional workers were required, Hudson Taylor and his associates spent protracted time in prayer until they received the assurance of faith that the number required would be granted. Both times, after an appeal for 70 new missionaries in 1880, and 100 in 1887, the full number reached China within the specified time and with all their support supplied.[61] A.T. Pierson is said to have exclaimed that, except for the prayers of praying mothers and fathers who prayed their children out to the mission field, there would have been no Student Volunteer Movement.

8. Prayer opens closed doors for occupation by a Christian presence.

The Apostle Paul urged the Christians of his generation, "Devote yourselves to prayer, being watchful and thankful. And pray for us too that God may open a door for our message so that we may proclaim the mystery of Christ" (Col.4:2-4).

A missionary friend recently gave me a striking illustration in this regard. Six years ago he visited the West African country of Guinea. Sekou Toure, a Marxist leader, had just kicked out all the missionaries except two, and was torturing political prisoners. The two remaining missionaries and twelve national pastors met with him to intercede for the country. First, they interceded with God for the removal of the Marxist tyrant who had closed the door to further mission efforts when most of the people groups still remained unoccupied by the church. Then they put up maps around the room in which they were meeting, and together laid their hands upon those areas of the country and groups that had no Christian presence. They prayed and agreed together for a breakthrough and the establishment of Christian ministries in them. Within a year, Sekou Toure was gone, replaced by a leader who opened the door to missions once again, and today every one of the people groups they prayed for are now occupied by a national or missionary effort.

In the past several years we have seen God open the anti-Christian bastions of Romania and Albania. Can we not expect Him to do the same with Mauritania, Morocco, Libya, Turkey, or Saudi Arabia, if God's people will focus their prayers on these difficult places? Can He not do the same with the particular people group you feel most concerned to reach?

When Jonathan Goforth planned to launch a new work in northern Honan Province in China, Hudson Taylor wrote to him with these words: "Brother, if you are to win that province, you must go forward on your knees."[62] His advice still holds today.

Prayer opens closed doors

9. **Aggressive praying or "spiritual warfare" praying breaks the control of the powers of darkness over people groups, cities and nations.**

There are also links that need to be broken if frontier missions are to go forward. Chains of spiritual darkness and bondage often link unreached peoples, cities and countries to principalities and powers who seek to control the affairs of humankind. At present in the missions world we are undergoing a rediscovery that the issue in reaching the unreached is one of spiritual power. Just as it was when Yahweh faced the gods of Egypt or Baal on Mount Carmel, so today the issue still is one of power encounter between the true God and false gods, those spirit beings who hold sway over segments of humanity.

Peter Wagner, in a symposium on power evangelism at Fuller Theological Seminary, affirmed:

> Satan delegates high-ranking members of the hierarchy of evil spirits to control nations, regions, cities, tribes, people groups, neighborhoods and other significant social networks of human beings throughout the world. Their major assignment is to prevent God from being glorified in their territory, which they do through directing the activity of lower-ranking demons.[63]

If Ephesians 6 indicates that all Christians are involved in an unseen warfare with the powers of darkness, how much more those of us who are involved in frontier missions as missionaries, intercessors, researchers or strategists? Paul says our struggle (literally "wrestling") is to be carried on through prayer in the Spirit. Apart from the sword of the Spirit, the word of God, prayer is the only offensive weapon available to us in this cosmic warfare.

Obviously, if we are going to see missionary breakthroughs in peoples, cities and countries, we will need to learn how to use the offensive weapon of prayer to dislodge the powers of darkness. While discussing the receptivity or resistance of people groups to Christ, Wagner draws out this implication: "It goes without saying that if this hypothesis concerning territorial spirits is correct, and if we could learn how to break their control through the power of God, positions on the resistance-receptivity axis could change virtually overnight."[64]

Francis Frangipane, writing about the strongholds the powers of darkness maintain over groups of people, takes a similar line of thinking:

> There are Satanic strongholds over countries and communities; there are strongholds which influence churches and individuals.... These fortresses exist in the thought patterns and ideas that govern individuals... as well as communities and nations. Before victory can be claimed, these strongholds must be pulled down, and Satan's armor removed. Then the mighty weapons of the Word and the Spirit can effectively plunder Satan's house.[65]

Studies of the belief systems of pagan peoples attest to the reality of the picture of spirit beings portrayed in Ephesians 6, the book of Daniel and elsewhere. The Burmese believe in supernatural beings called nats arranged hierarchically with control over natural phenomena, villages, regions and nations. Their link with these beings is maintained through witches or mediums, at least one of whom is found in each village.[66]

In Thailand there are both village and regional spirits, with the village ones being subordinate to the regional ones. Pillars are often erected in villages as a habitat for their guardian spirits.[67] One CMA missionary told me of the increasing oppression and lack of spiritual responsiveness she and her coworker encountered in a village once this pillar was erected. An OMF missionary believes he has identified the national principality over all of Thailand.

In India a similar cosmology involving guardian spirits over villages and others over regions is found. They are often associated with disease, sudden death and catastrophe.[68] Kali, the goddess of destruction, is a regional deity known especially among the Bengalis of West Bengal in Calcutta. Anyone who has been to Calcutta can see the devastating impact she and her worship have made upon that city and its people. Christian workers living there have complained of severe oppression and serious disunity in the churches. But recently they have come together to pray regularly for the city and to take offensive action against the powers of darkness. They are now beginning to see spiritual breakthroughs in several people groups, with new ministries developing and churches proliferating. It is a testimony to the powerful resource of united prayer by God's people.

A book on the African country of Zimbabwe reveals that every region, city, village is thought to be under the control of territorial spirits.69 In Nigeria an Assemblies of God leader, who formerly was a high-ranking occult practitioner before his conversion, said that Satan assigned him control of 12 spirits, each of which controlled 600 demons. He testified, "I was in touch with all the spirits controlling each town in Nigeria, and I had a shrine in all the major cities."[70]

Recently in a meeting with a well-known Japanese evangelist and several missionaries to Japan, I was surprised to discover how much the Japanese are still bound up with occultism. We can be fooled by the highly technological, modern look of Japan, and not realize that large numbers of the Japanese still attend Shinto shrines, that every school child carries an amulet, or that Shinto priests are called upon to dedicate each new building. And a dangerous phenomenon is now facing us in the West as New Age cults advocate "channeling" to communicate with spirit beings, thus reestablishing links with the powers of darkness originally broken by the evangelization and Christianization of Western societies.

The problem is that most of us do not realize we are in a no-holds-barred war, and therefore, we may feel no need for prayer as a powerful resource. John Piper, a Minneapolis pastor, puts it this way:

> The problem is that most Christians don't really believe that life is war, and that our invisible enemy is awesome. How then are you ever going to get them to pray? They'll say they believe these truths, but watch their lives. There is a peace-time casualness in the church about spiritual things. There are no bombs falling in their lives, no bullets whizzing overhead, no mines to avoid, no roars on the horizon.... So why pray?[71]

In Mark 3:27, Jesus said something that is especially relevant to the activity of frontier missions: "No one can enter a strongman's house and carry off his possessions unless he first ties up the strongman. Then he can rob his house." It stands to reason that we as missionaries cannot be successful in entering and carrying off what has belonged to Satan for centuries—portions of humanity under his dominion—without binding the territorial spirits that have delegated control there. Prayer in the Spirit, informed by facts uncovered by research, is a potent force in binding the strongmen over cities, people groups and countries. Again John

Demons downtown

Dawson's book demonstrates how research can uncover a community's link with the powers of darkness, and united prayer in the Spirit can break that link.

In Matthew 18:18-19, Jesus gave a startling assurance to those who pray in this way: "I tell you the truth, whatever you bind on earth will be bound in heaven, and whatever you loose on earth will be loosed in heaven. Again I tell you, that if two of you on earth agree about anything you ask for, it will be done for you by my father in heaven." Effective spiritual warfare occurs when we pray in unity with others. This teaching demonstrates the importance of prayer groups and networks being formed where people pray prayers of agreement for certain people groups, cities or countries in an in-depth way. This, it seems to me, is what will bring the breakthrough.

The Greek word for "bind" in these verses means "to chain or imprison." The prayers of God's people joined together will chain and circumscribe the activity of spirit beings that are hostile to the glory of God and the expansion of His kingdom on earth. As the Apostle Paul puts it, "The weapons we fight with are not the weapons of the world. On the contrary, they have divine power to demolish strongholds" (II Corinthians 10:3-4).

The experience of Omar Cabrera, a pastor and evangelist in Argentina, underlines the awesome weaponry that prayer in the Spirit brings to bear on the occult realm. Over the past several years, he has made it his practice to fast and pray for a number of days before opening an evangelism campaign in a city he is trying to reach.

Often during those periods of fasting and prayer, spirit beings will come against him, even appearing in grotesque shapes, to contest his presence and his plan to evangelize that city. They often say, "You have no right to be here. This is my territory." To which he replies, "On the contrary, you have no right to be here. I bind you in the authority of Jesus Christ, the one who has all authority in heaven and on earth." Immediately that spirit flees the scene and a higher principality will often come into place against Cabrera.

In the same way, through a struggle in prayer, Cabrera breaks the hold of that being which often turns out to be a spirit of witchcraft. When the topmost strongman is bound, the mood of the whole city

"In the name of Jesus, get out of our city!"

changes—often from one of resistance to the gospel, to one of great receptivity—with hundreds and thousands coming to Christ, accompanied by extraordinary signs and wonders, healings and miracles. Using this approach, Cabrera has gone from ministering to a congregation of under 20, to being the pastor of the world's third largest church with over 140,000.

As outlandish as Cabrera's experiences may seem, we would do well to apply what he and many other Christian workers are learning about prayer warfare to the work of frontier missions. As I have traveled to many countries leading consultations and seminars on mission strategy for national Christian workers, the issue of spiritual warfare keeps coming up. My growing conviction is that in many resistant contexts we can strategize and evangelize until we are blue in the face with no effect until we identify and bind the strongman over the group we are seeking to reach. Until this happens we are unlikely to see much of a response.

Could it be that whole peoples we have written off as being "resistant" are in themselves really not resistant at all, but are in the grip of spirit beings that are the source of the resistance? Arthur Matthews writes of his burden in intercession for two specific areas of Southeast Asia where the missionaries were unable to make headway: "So asserting my position with Christ in the heavenlies on the basis of God's word, I took unto me the whole armor of God in order to stand against the wiles of the devil, and to withstand his opposition to the gospel." He held on until news from both places began to change: "The resisting powers in both places were weakened, making possible victories for the Lord."[72]

Loren Cunningham, general director of Youth With A Mission, describes his experience in praying and fasting for three days with 12 coworkers in 1973. As they prayed the Lord revealed they should pray for the downfall of the "prince of Greece." On the same day in New Zealand and Europe, YWAM groups received a similar word from God. All three groups obeyed and came against this principality. Within 24 hours, a political coup changed the government of Greece, bringing greater freedom for mission activity in the country.[73]

While I was in Senegal conducting a seminar, an Assemblies of God mission leader told me their denomination had begun to pray and fast corporately for the Muslims. They are now seeing a new responsiveness of these people, and churches are being established among them.

The Challenge of Linking the Global Prayer Movement with Frontier Missions

David Barrett and Todd Johnson in their book *Our Globe and How to Reach It* estimate there are 22 active global prayer movements in existence. Certainly we rejoice in the resurgence of prayer in the worldwide church; however, there is little evidence that these prayer movements are linked directly enough with the unevangelized world. The Lausanne Global Prayer Strategy for world evangelization is one example. Although Christians from many countries are involved in praying for world evangelization each morning as a new day dawns, the focus of prayer is quite general with no move as yet being made to link these intercessors with specific segments of the unevangelized world or to feed them with updated information so that their prayers will be more specific and effectual.

The Concerts of Prayer movement is a similar example. It provides an excellent introduction to getting people praying for spiritual revival and world evangelization, but it needs to get participants tied in with specific people groups, cities or nations for more in-depth, persevering and informed prayer. Even the call to prayer, issued by the 1984 Seoul Congress on Prayer and World Evangelization, though it emphasized the importance of prayer and spiritual warfare, gave no indication of how this kind of praying could be tied to the unevangelized world in a practical, ongoing way.

There are enormous prayer resources within the body of Christ that by and large are not being tapped for the unevangelized world because we have thus far failed to develop practical mechanisms to link these resources with the need of the unreached. For example, at the Indianapolis 1990 Congress on the Holy Spirit and World Evangelization, no one from the plenary shared any of the facts concerning the unevangelized world with the 20,000 participants, nor did we stop to pray for particular segments of that world. This was a glaring oversight.

Nevertheless, there are some good models which suggest it is possible to get Christians linked up with particular people groups, cities and countries by feeding them with ongoing information so that they will be able to hold on like bulldogs until the breakthrough occurs. The "strategic coordinator" approach, which the Southern Baptists have pioneered, is noteworthy. One strategic coordinator for an ethnic minority of China has managed to get 500 churches praying for this people group. He has researched the people thoroughly and kept the intercessors informed. Now thousands are coming to Christ, and a breakthrough is on the way.

The Global Prayer Digest published by the Frontier Fellowship of the U.S. Center for World Mission is another fine example of a practical mechanism which links praying Christians with unreached people groups. The Adopt-A-People program, now an international movement, also has great potential for linking praying congregations with particular people groups.

I am convinced more than ever that unless prayer networks come into being, focused on each of the 2,000 or so major unreached peoples, world evangelization by AD 2000 or any time will be just a pipe-dream. As we have seen, the battle must be won in the spiritual realm if Christian workers are to occupy the territory and reap the harvest. Like assault troops landing on an enemy beach, they will need a prayer bombardment to knock out enemy positions before they are able to occupy that people group or city in need of Christ. George Peters, the late missiologist, wrote:

> We have become in missions so wrapped up in technology and methodology that we have forgotten that missions is number one, the releasing of divine dynamics.... Reaching the unreached will, first of all, mean for us not only to lay hold of it in faith, but to develop thousands and thousands of prayer cells that will commit themselves wholeheartedly to prayer until the victory will be won.[74]

Along with Peters, I believe that probably the most strategic thing we can do for frontier missions is to stimulate the formation of ongoing prayer and spiritual warfare networks focused on particular unreached peoples. They will become those watchmen on the wall who will never be silent day or night until, as Isaiah says, God makes that segment of humanity "a praise in the earth" and until those people will be called "the holy people, the redeemed of the Lord" (Isaiah 62:1-12). David Bryant puts it this way:

> The greatest challenge any of us will ever face in the global cause of Christ [and] "the greatest contribution any of us will ever make to the glorious task of advancing Christ's Kingdom among earth's unreached is... to grow as men and women of prayer and to mobilize others with us into a movement of prayer for the world." Other things wait to be done but this is the greatest.[75]

QUESTIONS FOR REFLECTION
AND DISCUSSION

How can we stimulate the formation of prayer networks for the unreached peoples in our nation?

_____

_____

_____

_____

How can they be kept going, supplied with up-to-date information so they don't lose interest and discontinue praying?

_____

_____

_____

_____

Do we have any other effective models of prayer and information sharing already in operation that can be shared?

_____

_____

_____

_____

How can the growing national and global prayer movements be more closely linked with specific unreached peoples in our nation?

_____

_____

_____

_____

Suggest some practical steps that need to be taken and an operational mechanism that can be set up.

- What agencies or individuals should be responsible?

_____

_____

_____

_____

- What can I do to develop a local prayer effort for the people group I am most concerned to reach for Christ?

_____

_____

_____

_____

MATTERS FOR PRAYER

- Pray for any unreached peoples you are aware of or specially concerned for as the Holy Spirit brings them to mind. Pray for the breaking of the hold of principalities and powers, liberation to receive Christ and for Christian workers and ministries among them.

- Pray for the development of ongoing prayer networks for every remaining unreached people, that God will raise up intercessors with a special burden for each segment of the unevangelized world.

- Ask for God's guidance in the implementation of the ideas you have conceived. What should you do? How can you work with others to develop prayer efforts focused on the unreached peoples in your area?

Part Four

NETWORKING THE WHOLE CHURCH

Networks link Christian
workers for outreach

The Chinese have been around for a long time, with a civilization stretching back 5000 years. In that time they have developed a lot of wisdom about life and particularly human relationships in society. An ancient Chinese proverb goes like this:

> Heaven and Hell are exactly alike in that each is an enormous banquet with every wonderful dish imaginable crowding the great round table. The diners are provided with chopsticks five feet long.

> In Hell the diners give up struggling to feed themselves with these impossible tools and sit in ravenous frustration.

> In Heaven everyone feeds the person across the table.

Though its theology is a bit strange, this proverb is so right in affirming that there is something heavenly about cooperation, about human beings depending on one another and serving one another in relationships that benefit everyone concerned. However, in our efforts to reach unreached peoples we Christian leaders often look more like the picture of those sitting in "ravenous frustration" trying to go it alone in our independence and isolation from one another.

The main problem: lack of collaboration

David Barrett and James Reapsome in their book *Seven Hundred Plans to Evangelize the World* identified lack of cooperation and collaboration between Christian organizations as the major hindrance to world evangelization. They write that two-thirds of all global evangelization plans are stand-alone, self-sufficient plans, each viewing itself as at the center of world evangelization. They estimate that 96 percent of all global evangelization plans ignore or write off all other Christian traditions with which they are not like-minded and *only four percent* seek to network or connect meaningfully with those of other Christian traditions.[76] Their conclusion is:

"The absence of any network is catastrophic. It is probably the major single cause of the fiasco of today's unevangelized world... largely untouched from one year to the next."[77]

The Global Consultation on World Evangelization by AD 2000 and Beyond held in Singapore at the beginning of January 1989 also recognized this problem. The Great Commission Manifesto prepared by over 300 leaders from a wide diversity of Christian traditions stated:

We see afresh that cooperation and partnership are absolute necessities if the Great Commission is going to be fulfilled by the year 2000. For the sake of those who are lost and eternally separated from God, we have dared to pray and dream of what might happen if appropriate autonomy of churches and ministries could be balanced with significant partnership.[78]

The major hindrance to world evangelization is lack of cooperation and collaboration between Christian organizations

In a pre-consultation survey of key Christian leaders around the world, 70 percent affirmed that reaching unreached peoples was the key to fulfilling the Great Commission. Picking up that affirmation, the Manifesto enunciated the following goals, all of which focus on reaching unreached peoples:

- Focus particularly on those who have not yet heard the gospel.
- Provide every people and population on earth with a valid opportunity to hear the gospel in a

language they can understand. It is our fervent prayer that at least half of humanity will profess allegiance to the Lord Jesus.

■ Establish a mission-minded church planting movement within every unreached people group so that the gospel is accessible to all people.

■ Establish a Christian community of worship, instruction in the Word, healing, fellowship, prayer, disciple making, evangelism, and missionary concern in every human community.[79]

These are all marvelous, worthy goals that most likely we will support and work to attain. However, if we are to stand a chance of achieving such glorious, grandiose goals, we must give much more attention to the practical, nitty-gritty matter of how we can *cooperate* in reaching unreached peoples. Unless we find a way to move *together* toward these goals by building effective partnerships between Christian organizations, the idea of reaching the estimated remaining 2,000 major unreached peoples and their thousands of subgroups by AD 2000 is a mirage that will quickly disappear.

How can we develop relationships that will both *maintain the autonomy* of individual churches and parachurch organizations as well as *make possible significant partnership*? I suggest that it will be through *building networks* focused on reaching unreached peoples.

What is networking?

"Networks" and "networking" are terms that have come into recent prominence, first in the social protest movement as a way of mobilizing massive grassroots involvement in causes such as the anti-nuclear movement, women's rights and environmental protection. Later, they entered the vocabulary of business and industry, meaning the sharing of information and ideas in a more informal, open manner to enhance greater creativity and productivity in the workplace.[80] Japanese management and production units built on the network concept have shown the world how exceedingly productive a social structure it can be.

John Naisbitt, the author of the best-selling book *Megatrends*, says that one of the major trends of our time is movement away from hierarchal social structures with top-down, pyramid-like, organization to more informal, flexible, horizontal networks that can bring people together to accomplish practically any shared goal. Probably for this reason, the network has been called "the most rapidly growing form of social organization in the world."[81]

Networks and networking are not new concepts. One anthropologist calls the network the "oldest social invention," since many pre-industrial societies have organized themselves in this way. For example, those who have sought to conquer the squabbling, seemingly divided tribes of Arabia have been amazed by their rapid ability to coalesce into a unified fighting force.[82] Also, Japanese management and production unit structure likely have their roots in the village tradition of all

NETWORKING TO
REACH THE UNREACHED

neighbors uniting to help each other bring in the rice harvest.

Even scientific research seems to affirm that networking is part and parcel of nature itself. In what is called "the New Physics," the whole universe is seen by physicists as "an interconnected network, an indivisible whole."[83]

But what is a "network"? According to the dictionary it is, physically speaking, "a fabric or structure of cords or wires that cross at regular intervals and are knotted or secured at the crossings."[84] This physical picture is helpful for us in conceiving of a network from the social point of view. Socially speaking, a network is any number of individuals or organizations linked together by a *commitment to shared values*.[85] "Networking" is that process by which individuals or organizations become connected with one another to achieve particular common goals.

Authors Jessica Lipnack and Jeffrey Stamps describe networking in this way:

A network is a web of free standing participants cohering through shared values and interest. Networking is people connecting with people, linking ideas and resources. One person with a need contacts another with a resource and networking begins.[86]

Advantages of networking

As a social structure, networking has numerous advantages:

- It enables individuals and organizations to maintain a balance between autonomy on the one hand and dependence on the other.[87] From the standpoint of world evangelization, it makes interdenominational cooperation more feasible because participants do not have to forsake commitment to their organizations to take part. Network boundaries are fluid and open rather than rigid and closed.

- Its segmented, decentralized structure permits leadership to be shared by its members. They relate as equals rather than as subordinates to superiors.[88]

- It facilitates horizontal, free-flowing communication among all participants, making possible more creative, innovative responses in a synergistic manner. It promotes the flow of ideas even across cultural and organizational barriers.[89]

■ It is a flexible, mobile and low-profile structure, making it ideal for rapidly changing situations and for politically restrictive societies. This advantage makes the network model ideal for reaching unreached peoples, most of whom now reside in limited or restricted access nations, many with repressive regimes. If one segment is closed down or imprisoned, the rest of the network continues to function. The church in China has functioned like this for decades. Shared leadership and the decentralized, segmented nature of the house-church movement makes it impossible for the state to control or shut the movement down completely.

■ It is inexpensive, since there is no heavy administrative apparatus and control mechanism to support. People work together, volunteering their time on the basis of shared interest and vision.

Is it biblical?

Some of us may be put off by the terms "network" and "networking" since they come from secular usage and sound rather technological. But all truth is God's truth, and if so might we not expect to find some biblical parallels for these concepts?

Luke Chapter 5 is one place to start. The practice of using nets at Christ's direction to pull in an astonishing catch of fish leads to Jesus' assertion that the disciples will soon be catching men. During that episode they not only learn the importance of going in obedience to Jesus where the fish are, but also the need for *partnership* in bringing in a catch that is more than anyone can handle alone. They also learn that by *working the nets together* under the direction of Christ, they can expect Him to work wonders through their united efforts.

Later in Acts 2 Peter preaches that famous sermon that brings 3000 to Christ—a phenomenal response. However, we need to see what is behind that response. It is interesting to note the words of Scripture "But Peter *standing with the eleven* lifted up his voice..." This is not a one-man show! There is a unity of heart and mind brought about not only by working and learning together during the ministry of Christ, but afterwards cemented by their regular meeting and praying together mentioned in Acts 1. Their hearts are knit together, their lives interwoven like strands into a net Christ can use to sweep thousands into His Kingdom.

This *interconnectedness* is a well-known theme throughout the New Testament. Paul emphasizes the oneness of the body of Christ, a unity made up of many interdependent parts. It is a body in which one part cannot say to another "I have no need for you" because all are gifted in different ways and have a vital contribution to make to the whole. This is an emphasis we need to rediscover in the wider mission community with our common tendency to go it alone, competing with one another for the donor dollar, promoting our own organizations, ministries and agendas rather than working unitedly to reach unreached peoples.

Have you ever been struck as I have by the lack of direct admonitions by Paul and the other apostles in their epistles to evangelize the unreached? The priority in apostolic teaching instead was clearly on maintaining and building up the interconnectedness of God's people. Why is this the case? Certainly because Paul and the other apostles realized that strong relationships between Christians communicating and receiving love and truth, joined together as ligaments in a body would fit them to serve as a gigantic net that Christ could use to haul in the unreached.

Indeed in Ephesians 4, Paul mixes the two metaphors of the net and body. There he uses the Greek term for *mending nets* to describe how the four-fold ministries of apostles, prophets, evangelists and pastor-teachers equip or *mend* God's people for works of service for the building up of the body of Christ. He knew that mending people in their relationships to God and other believers would more than anything else enable the church to catch the unbelieving world for the Kingdom. Jesus also prayed that we as Christians might be *one*, joined together in complete unity so that the world might believe that the Father sent Him.

We have been hearing in the news about the use of drift nets by trawlers in the North Pacific and the outrage environmentalists feel at the use of those nets. Fifty feet high, miles long and made of tough nylon filament that cannot be ruptured, frayed or broken, they are literal vacuum cleaners, sweeping every living creature into their grasp. This image which is negative to some, positively shows us the possibilities of Christian networking in the power of the Spirit to sweep the unreached into the Kingdom.

Getting practical

Given the awesome potential of networks and networking for advancing world evangelization, practically speaking how can we go about building such structures to reach unreached peoples?

1. *We can build networks around particular ministries.* "The World by 2000" is a prime example of the way in which three missions leaders—the presidents of HCJB, FEBC and TWR—formed a network to coordinate their radio broadcasting efforts. By the year 2000 they plan to make sure that every individual on earth can hear the gospel by radio in a language he or she can understand.

In 1985, these three leaders simply got together for a time of prayer and sharing their visions. They made an agreement to begin a process of cooperation that has resulted in an end of competition and duplication of efforts so that they can work together to broadcast the gospel in far more languages of unreached peoples that have never had Christian broadcasts before.[90]

Many different kinds of opportunities on both the global level and the in-country level exist for networking around particular ministries.

2. However, the kind of networking I want to emphasize here is that which occurs when two, three or more Christian leaders decide they want to cooperate interdenominationally *to reach a particular unreached people group.* Over and over again, especially in the last several years, we have witnessed the power and potential of

this kind of process to impact people groups with the gospel.

Simply by starting with two to three others who share your vision for reaching a particular segment of the population and meeting to pray together, listen to one another and coordinate your plans, opens the door for God to do wonders. The Bible says "one shall chase a thousand, but two shall put 10,000 to flight." There is a *synergism* by which two or more working together are ten times more potent, because in the power of the Spirit $1 + 1 = 10$!

Too often we allow denominational and organizational barriers to keep us from linking up with others on the basis of *shared vision* for evangelizing a particular group or groups. As a result our interconnections are weak and more on an official basis than on a visionary, spiritual one.

In the past nine years it has been my deep privilege to facilitate Unreached Peoples Strategy Consultations for Christian leaders in many countries around the world. During the course of getting leaders together to think, pray and develop common strategies, a similar pattern has been repeated many times over. When Christian leaders who normally would not associate with one another (except on an occasional basis) begin to pray and think together about their common concern for a group of people, something wonderful begins to happen. The Holy Spirit begins to knit them together so that at the end of their session, they often say to one another: "We have all been working independently of one another to reach the same group. Why don't we pool our efforts and resources to maximize our effectiveness?"

In Taiwan, this happened when 15 national workers and Western missionaries of different churches and organizations, all previously working independently to reach the Hakka people, decided to form an ongoing ministry network. They have continued to meet periodically over the years to pray, share lessons learned, and to coordinate their efforts. Together they have completed cultural research, published Scripture and hymnals, set up a vocational training program and, best of all, seen eighteen new fellowships of Hakka believers come into being, all led by indigenous leaders.

In Burundi, 25 denominational leaders and pastors decided to form an interdenominational network focussed on reaching the Pygmies, a people group that had seen many uncoordinated and unsuccessful prior efforts at evangelization.

These are just two examples of what God is doing by His Spirit to build John 17 unity among Christian agencies and leaders, so that working together as one, the world will know that Christ the Savior has been sent by the Father. In many multiplied instances the Holy Spirit is doing the same thing all around the world, breaking down those denominational, doctrinal and other barriers that have kept Christian workers separated and working independently of one another. Praise the Lord! This growing phenomenon bodes well for the reaching of other unreached peoples.

One practical way of building ministry networks that I have found to be useful, and that may be of use to you, is the Networking Through Consultation Model:

- Gather key leaders together.
- Talk about "people group" and "unreached people group" definitions and their meaning in your context. (See these definitions at the end of this chapter.)
- Assemble a list of local people groups and unreached people groups.
- Spend time in prayer to the Lord of the harvest for the groups listed (Matthew 9:36-38).
- Participants identify people groups they are reaching or want to reach.
- Collate participants' responses according to similar people groups identified.
- Get them into discussion groups to "network" with one another through thinking, praying and strategizing together on the basis of their common vision for reaching their people group.

The first step, gathering key Christian leaders together on a city basis or national basis, is not easy but is possible if the consultation is planned far enough in advance and held under broad enough auspices, such as that of the National Evangelical Fellowship or Council of Churches. During the course of the consultation we first emphasize the strategic advantages of focussing ministries on particular people groups and how God has been using the people group approach around the world. We also consider the Biblical stress on peoples and people groups rather than on political nations.

We use the definitions of "people group" and "unreached people group" that have come to be widely accepted in the Lausanne and AD 2000 movements for world evangelization. (See these definitions at the end of this chapter.) Participants are encouraged to look at their own society through this grid in order to identify as many distinct people groups as possible and designate those that are still unreached. It is often remarkable to see the surprised reactions of leaders who never realized how many diverse groups inhabited their country and how many have been neglected from the standpoint of Christian witness.

After identifying unreached people groups, we ask each participant to identify the particular people group he or she is already reaching or is burdened to reach. The responses are collected and participants put in discussion groups with others who chose the same group. They then seek to "network" with one another by discussing and praying through the answers to the following five questions:

1. What people group does God want you to reach?
2. What are they like?
3. Who should reach them?
4. How should they be reached?
5. What will be the result?

This is where the fun begins! The Holy Spirit seems to take over at this point and often brings to birth new ministry networks. It's exciting to watch Him work. I commend this approach to you as a way of multiplying ministry networks in your own area or nation.

Wouldn't it be wonderful to see a network of committed Christians come into being for every remaining unreached people group? I am convinced it is possible and must happen if world evangelization is to take place. We must work *together* to intentionally spawn thousands of new coalitions, task forces, *networks* focused on particular groups and also around particular ministries. It is a practical, doable way of catalyzing and carrying out evangelization of the unreached on both global and grass roots levels.

Conclusion

During a visit to an Asian country a few years ago I happened to stroll down to the harbor along with some local friends. As we ventured out on to one of its piers overlooking the water, we noticed a solitary woman fishing, hunched over a single pole, its line descending into the murky depths below. Glancing at her stony expression and the few, tiny fish swimming in the plastic bucket beside her, we asked how long she had been at it. "All day" was the dismayed reply, quickly adding even more gloomily, "I come most every day to catch some fish for my family's dinner or to sell in the market."

I wondered at the dedicated persistence of the woman, keeping at this unrewarding task in the hot sun day after day. "Would I be so committed?", I found myself reflecting inwardly. But my admiration of this rugged individual was short-lived. Gazing over the edge of the pier, I noticed hundreds, even thousands of fish darting back and forth in the shadows. And my wonderment at the lonely fisherwoman's dedication abruptly turned to astonishment at her stupidity. For if she had simply enlisted the help of a friend and together they lowered a net, she could have harvested a thousand times as much.

How often you and I in carrying out the Great Commission are like that woman, dedicated and persistent, yes, but in the final analysis, stupid and short sighted because we do not work closely with others engaged in the same task. We prefer to go it alone and settle for negligible results rather than work the nets together at Christ's direction to enjoy a spectacular catch for the Kingdom.

Through networking in the power and unity of His Spirit may we all become true "fishers of men"!

QUESTIONS FOR REFLECTION AND DISCUSSION

What other Christian workers from my own denomination and other denominations share my concern for reaching unreached peoples?

_____

_____

_____

_____

What steps need to be taken to build ministry networks focused on specific unreached peoples in our area? in our nation?

_____

_____

_____

_____

_____

_____

_____

_____

DEFINITIONS

People Group:

A significantly large grouping of individuals who perceive themselves to have a common affinity for one
another because of their shared:

> Language
> Religion
> Ethnicity
> Residence
> Occupation
> Class or caste
> Situation, etc.
> or combinations of these.

The largest group within which the gospel can flow
along natural lines without encountering barriers of
understanding or acceptance due to culture, language,
geography, etc.

Unreached People Group:

A people group among which there is no indigenous
community of believing Christians with adequate numbers and resources to evangelize this people group.

A Final Word

Congratulations! If you have worked through the exercises and thought through a long-range strategy for reaching a particular group of people, you are now a "people group thinker."

We would encourage you to keep and use this booklet as a reference manual for further planning and refining your strategy. The conditions of your people group as well as your own knowledge and experience will continually change, making it necessary for you to rethink your approach from time to time.

In any case, we would value your feedback as to what you are learning and how you are applying the people group paradigm in your ministry. Please send a copy of your research findings and ministry strategy to us at MARC. The information that you provide will greatly enhance our knowledge of people groups around the world and enable MARC to serve a networking function in informing others who can support you in prayer or partner with you in ministry. Of course, if you would prefer that we keep your information confidential, we will do that. In any case, let us hear from you at the address below.

Psalm 77:14 states: "You are the God who does wonders. You have revealed your power among the peoples." We may be confident that God will do his part as we move forward into his harvest among the unreached people groups of the world. Our strategizing, guided by research, broadened through networking and fueled by prayer, will position us for His mighty power's working through us to reach our target group.

Ephesians 3:20 gives us some indication of the awesome potential of that working through us. In our mission let us not only focus on the people group we hope to reach but also on our great God " who by the power at work within us is able to do far more abundantly than all that we ask or think."

Endnotes

Part one: *Focusing to reach unreached people groups*

1   See Harley Schreck and David Barrett, Unreached Peoples: Clarifying the Task (1986), published by MARC, for an extended discussion of the differences between ethnolinguistic peoples and sociologically defined people groups.

2   See Edward R. Dayton's That Everyone May Hear (1983 edition), published by MARC, for his discussion on this definition.

3   E. A. Speiser, The Anchor Bible: Genesis (New York: Doubleday, 1964), p. 86.

4   Richard Showalter, "All the Clans, All the Peoples" International Journal of Frontier Missions, Vol. 1, No. 2, 1984.

5   William L. Holladay, A Concise Hebrew and Aramaic Lexicon of the Old Testament (Grand Rapids: Eerdmans, 1971).

6   Francis Brown, S. R. Driver and Charles Briggs, A Hebrew and English Lexicon of the Old Testament (London: Oxford Press, 1968).

7   The results of the Consultation on the Relationship Between Evangelism and Social Responsibility are contained in the Lausanne Occasional Paper No. 21, "The Grand Rapids Report" (1982) and the book, In Word and Deed: Evangelism and Social Responsibility, edited by Bruce Nicholls (1985). Both are published jointly by the Lausanne Committee for World Evangelization and the World Evangelical Fellowship.

8   David B. Barrett, ed., World Christian Encyclopedia (Nairobi: Oxford University Press, 1982), p. 108.

9 Donald A. McGavran, Understanding Church Growth (Grand Rapids: Eerdmans, 1970), pp. 297-98.

10 Kenneth S. Latourette, Missions Tomorrow (New York: Harper, 1936), p. 159, quoted in McGavran, p. 298.

11 Quoted in James Engel, How Can I Get Them to Listen? (Grand Rapids: Zondervan, 1977), p. 23.

12 Gerald Hursh-Cesar and Prodipto Roy, ed., Third World Surveys: Survey Research in Developing Nations (Delhi: MacMillan, 1976), p. 62.

13 Donald E. Douglas, "Research for Ministry," an unpublished paper done at MARC, August 26, 1985.

14 Edward R. Dayton and David A. Fraser, Planning Strategies for World Evangelization (Grand Rapids: Eerdmans, 1980), p. 16.

15 Anatol Rapoport, ed. Clausewitz on War (Penguin, 1968), p. 83.

16 Viggo Søgaard, Applying Christian Communication (Fuller Theological Seminary, School of World Mission, PhD. Dissertation, 1986), pp. 225-63.

Part two: Practical procedures for people group thinking

17 Quoted by Bryant L. Myers in "For People, By People", World Vision Magazine, November 1982.

18 Judy Hutchinson, "Of Mirrors and Dragons" Together: A Journal of World Vision International, No. 13, Oct-Dec 1986, p. 27.

19 Edward R. Dayton, That Everyone May Hear: Workbook (Monrovia: MARC, 1986).

20 For a fuller treatment of PEP, including helpful photographs of PEP sessions in progress, see the series of articles in World Vision International's Journal Together (Oct-Dec 1983, Jan-Mar 1984, Apr-Jun 1984, Jul-Sept 1984 and Oct-Dec 1986).

21 Bronislaw Malinowski, Argonauts of the Western Pacific (London: Routledge, 1922), p. 25, quoted in James P. Spradley Participant Observation (New York: Holt, Rinehart and Winston, 1980), p. 3.

22 James P. Spradley and David W. McCurdy Anthropology: The Cultural Perspective (New York: Wiley, 1975), p. 46 and Spradley Participant Observation, pp. 6-11.

23 Spradley, Participant Observation, p. 54f.

24 Conrad M. Arensberg, Social Change: A Manual for Community Development (New York: Aldine Pub. Co. 1971) pp. 241-43.

25 Michael Q. Patton, Practical Evaluation (Beverly Hills: Sage Publications 1982), p. 161.

26 Patton, pp. 166-68.

27 Ibid.

28 Gerald Hursh-Cesar and Prodipto Ray, ed., Third World Surveys: Survey Research in Developing Nations (Delhi: MacMillan Company of India, 1976), p. 287f.

29 Howard Freeman, Peter Rossi and Sonya Wright, Evaluating Social Projects in Developing Countries (Paris: Development Center of Organization for Economic Cooperation and Development, 1979), pp. 60-61

30 Hursh-Cesar and Roy, p. 56

31 Arensberg, pp. 238-40.

32 Anne Hope and Sally Timmel, Training for Transformation: A Handbook for Community Workers, Book 1 (Harare, Zimbabwe: Mambo Press, 1984), pp. 35, 39-40.

33 Engel, pp. 81f.

34 James P. Spradley, Ethnographic Interviewing, pp. 86-87.

35 Ibid., pp. 87-88.

36 Patton, p. 179.

Part three: Releasing God's power through prayer

37 Mrs. J. O. Fraser, Fraser and Prayer (London: Missionary Fellowship, 1963), pp. 11-12.

38 Ibid., p. 26.

39 Ibid., pp. 46-47.

40 O. Hallesby, Prayer (London: InterVarsity Press, 1948) p. 67.

41 Quoted in Todd Johnson, Countdown to 1900: World Evangelization at the End of the 19th Century (Birmingham: New Hope, 1988) p. 37.

42 Ibid., p. 67.

43 Jonathan Goforth, By My Spirit, (New York: Harper and Brothers, 1930) pp. 188-189.

44 Robert H. Glover, The Bible Basis of Missions, (Chicago: Moody, 1946) p. 185.

45 Arthur Mathews, Born for Battle, (Robesonia, Pennsylvania: Overseas Missionary Fellowship, 1978), p. 42

46 Derek Prince, Shaping History through Prayer and Fasting, (Old Tappan, New Jersey: Flemming Revell Company, 1973), pp. 93, 95.

47 Goforth, p. 182.

48 F. Deavville Walker, William Carey, (Chicago: Moody Press, 1980), p. 52.

49 Glover, p. 178.

50 Ibid., p. 180.

51 Glover, p. 182

52 Ibid., pp. 180-181.

53 J. Edwin Orr, The Flaming Tongue: The Impact of 20th Century Revivals (Chicago: Moody Press, 1973), p. xiii.

54 Ibid., pp. x-xi.

55 David Bryant, "Prayer Movements Signal New Light for the Nations," Evangelical Missions Quarterly, (April 1987), p. 121.

56 Francis McGaw, Praying Hyde (Minneapolis: Bethany Fellowship, 1970).

57 Ibid.

58 Glover, p. 181.

59 Goforth, p. 184.

60 Ibid., pp. 184-185.

61 Glover, p. 183.

62 Quoted in Wesley Duewel, Mighty Prevailing Prayer, (Grand Rapids: Francis Asbury Press, 1990), p. 250.

63 Peter Wagner, "Territorial Spirits," Academic Symposium on Power Evangelism, Fuller Seminary, December 13-15, 1988, pp. 3-4.

64 Ibid.

65 Francis Frangipane, The Three Battlegrounds, (Marion, Iowa, River of Life Ministries, 1989), pp. 15,21.

66 Melford Spiro, Burmese Supernaturalism.

67 S. J. Pambiah, Buddhism and the Spirit Cults in Northeast Thailand, 1970.

68 David Kinsley, The Sword and the Flute, 1975.

69 From a conversation with Jim Montgomery of DAWN Ministries, 1605 Elizabeth Street, Pasadena, CA 91104.

70 Wagner, p. 4.

71 John Piper, "Prayer: The Power that Wields the Weapon," Mission Frontiers, June-July, 1989, p. 15.

72 Duewel, p. 248.

73 Wagner, p. 10.

74 Quoted in Bryant, p. 118.

75 Ibid.

Part four: Networking the whole church

76 Barrett, David B. and Reapsome, James W., Seven Hundred Plans to Evangelize the World (Birmingham, Alabama: New Hope, 1988), pp. 49-50.

77 Ibid.

78 Wang, Thomas, ed. Countdown to AD 2000 (Pasadena, CA: AD 2000 Movement, Inc., 1989), p. xii.

79 Ibid, pp. xii-xiii.

80 Gilroy, Norm and Swan, Jim, Building Networks!: Cooperation as a Strategy for Success in a Changing World (San Francisco, CA: Kendall Hunt Publishing Co., 1983), p. 12.

81 Ibid., pp. 12, 31.

82 McInnis, Noel, "Networking: A Way to Change the World?" The Futurist (June 1984), p. 9.

83 Gilroy and Swan, p. 7.

84 Webster's New Collegiate Dictionary (Springfield, MA: G. & C. Merriam Co., 1981).

85 Lipnack, Jessica and Stamps, Jeffrey, "A Network Model" The Futurist (July - August, 1987), p. 23. They quote Virginia Hine's article in The Futurist (June 1984).

86 Lipnack, Jessica and Stamps, Jeffrey, The Networking Book: People Connecting With People (New York: Routledge Kegan Paul, 1986), pp. 2-3.

87 See Lipnack and Stamps "A Network Model," pp. 23-24, for an excellent discussion on this.

88 Ibid.

89 See Gilroy and Swan, p. 12, for a fuller exposition of network model advantages.

90 See a full account of this story in Wang, Countdown to 2000, entitled "World by 2000: A Journey of Cooperation."

Questionnaire

People Group Identification

Name of the people group: _____

Country where located: _____

Approximate size of group in this country: _____

Religion(s) of People Group

Religion	% Adherents	% Practicing
CHRISTIAN		
Protestant		
Roman Catholic		
Other		
NON-CHRISTIAN		
TOTAL FOR ALL CATEGORIES	100%	100%

Christian Witness to this People Group

If there are Christian churches or missions (national or foreign) now active within the area or region where this group is concentrated, please use the following table to list the name of church, mission or denomination, the year work began in this area, the approximate number of full members from this people group, the approximate number of adherents including children, and the approximate number of trained pastors and evangelists from this group. (If there are none, check here ☐)

Church or Mission	Year	Members	Adherents	Workers

In your opinion, what is the attitude of this people group toward Christianity?

☐ Strongly favorable   ☐ Somewhat opposed
☐ Somewhat favorable   ☐ Strongly opposed
☐ Indifferent

What is the growth rate of the total Christian community among this people group?

☐ Rapid growth   ☐ Slow decline
☐ Slow growth   ☐ Rapid decline
☐ Stable

People Group Language

Please list the various languages or dialects used by the members of this people group:

Language type	Primary name (s)	% who speak	% who read
Vernacular/ common language			
Lingua Franca/trade language			

Other Information

What are the felt needs of this people group (meaning in life, freedom from demonic oppression, food, housing, healthcare, or others)?

_____

_____

_____

_____

_____

_____

_____

How could this group best be reached? What means and methods of ministry would be most effective in meeting their needs?

_____

_____

_____

_____

_____

_____

_____

Questionnaire completed by:

Name: _____ Date: _____

Organization: _____

Address: _____

Please send this completed questionnaire to:

MARC
800 West Chestnut Avenue
Monrovia, CA 91016-3198
U.S.A.